CHEE CHEE

McGill-Queen's Native and Northern Series
Bruce G. Trigger, Editor

CHEE CHEE

A Study of Aboriginal Suicide

AL EVANS

McGill-Queen's University Press

Montreal & Kingston • London • Ithaca

© McGill-Queen's University Press 2004
ISBN 0-7735-2687-0

Legal deposit second quarter 2004
Bibliothèque nationale du Québec

Printed in Canada on acid-free paper

This book has been published with the help of
a grant from St Paul's United Church.

Poetry by Rita Joe and Lillian Sugabaquelol is
published by permission of the authors.
Photograph on title page by Ernie Bies, 1976.

The author has made every effort to contact
individuals whose work is reprinted here.
Notice of any errors or omissions in this regard
will be gratefully received and correction made
in any subsequent edition.

McGill-Queen's University Press acknowledges
the financial support of the Canada Council
for the Arts for our publishing program. We
also acknowledge the financial support of the
Government of Canada through the Book Publishing Industry Development Program
(BPIDP) for our publishing activities.

National Library of Canada Cataloguing
in Publication

Evans, Al, 1920–
Chee Chee : a study of Canadian aboriginal
suicide / Al Evans.
Includes bibliographical references and index.
ISBN 0-7735-2687-0

1. Chee Chee, Benjamin, 1944–1977. 2. Native
peoples–Canada–Suicidal behavior–Case
studies. I. Title.

ND249.C415E92 2004
362.28'092
C2003-905943-X

For Benjamin Chee Chee's mother,
Josephine Chee Chee Roy,

and his great friend
Frederick C. Brown

CONTENTS

FOREWORD

When Alvin Evans introduced himself to me a few years ago, one of the topics he raised was the need for discussion about Canadian Aboriginal suicide. Al was researching this area because of his professional training, but he was specifically interested in the life and death of Benjamin Chee Chee. His question was how a non-Aboriginal could respectfully engage himself in this story.

Some months ago, we met again with new developments to reflect upon. Contact with family and friends had made it possible for him to begin writing this book with integrity. He was absolutely convinced of the need to present information about the phenomenon of self-destructive behaviour in Aboriginal communities.

The arrival of the new millennium has not ended the struggles of the past century. Canadian Aboriginal Peoples who have lived in the twentieth century have many unresolved painful memories. The continued marginalization of peoples and the oppressive nature of our aggressive society does isolate victims. Many of the Aboriginal Peoples who experience life on the fringe of society feel victimized. Colonial history and the story of first contact indicate an early awareness of the loss of hope. A Mayan writer tells of the sickness that came with the foreigners and caused him to despair: "Therefore let us perish for our Gods are already dead!"

The loss of creative options and the captivity of Aboriginal Peoples in a cycle of increasing dependency on governmental charity has been the result of an ill-conceived plan. The intent was to develop structures that would force integration and assimilation of Aboriginal Peoples. Governments did not take into account the inherent racism in society and its institutions that would deny Aboriginal Peoples a place in the societal framework. Nor did the social manipulators realize how resistant to change Aboriginal cultures would be. Assimilation has not occurred.

Suicidal behaviour has become a problem for many Aboriginal communities in Canada, and it is increasingly youth focused. Many villages have experienced people in their teen years committing or attempting suicide. A pattern of three or four teen deaths in succession would suggest that suicide pacts are being made. This also reveals a prevailing atmosphere of despair among the young adults in many Aboriginal communities.

Benjamin Chee Chee lived with anger and frustration for more than thirty years before he took his life. The urgency to get at the work of prevention is included in Evans's experience, but my interest in this book comes from knowing how young people are today when they contemplate suicide. In 1989 I was invited to spend some time with a class of grade 5 students because a ten year-old-classmate had hung himself in a closet of the urban apartment block. He was the eldest of five children and had demonstrated academic and social giftedness. Yet there was something in his life that this Aboriginal child could not accept.

There has been a long history of frustration around education and employment opportunities for Aboriginal Peoples. Many young people find the process of education degrading and drop out in their early teens. Even those who succeed in academic pursuits often find the process irrelevant. The possibility of employment is low for Aboriginal youth, and many communities have gangs of young people who may be a threat to themselves and to their community.

This book about Aboriginal suicide is relevant to the current experiences of our society. Evans brings to our attention the story of a gifted artist who died in an institution. The Ottawa jail is like many others that are filled with Aboriginal youth. Statistics show that the situation has worsened since the death of Benjamin Chee Chee. More people who are Aboriginal are incarcerated now than in the 1970s, and the social disintegration has continued. The levels of unemployment and poverty have continued to rise, and the dynamic of displaced Aboriginal populations is shaking the structures of many urban communities.

The reflection on ways of healing for Aboriginal Peoples has been sustained by individual elders. These women and men have continued to remind us of the teachings which are about the good life. Alvin Evans refers to the drum beat as a calling of Aboriginal Peoples to rediscovery of their spiritual roots. There are obvious signs of hope in the increasing numbers who attend ceremonies and find strength in cultural learnings.

Governments and churches are setting aside resources for healing. The question is: Is this too little, too late? If the healing can be recognized as a dynamic process that is necessary for non-Aboriginals as well, then we may find health after all.

We have the potential to address the challenges of Canadian Aboriginal suicide. The information about root causes and prevention is accessible. With the *Royal Commission Report on Aboriginal Peoples* and the extensive historic research that has been completed across this country, it is time to be proactive around the issues related to Aboriginal suicide. Evans offers a framework for the reflection necessary to initiate education and programs for Canadian society. The life of Benjamin Chee Chee can serve as a focus for our creative involvement in healing for each of us and for our communities.

Rt. Rev. Dr Stan McKay
Past Moderator, The United Church of Canada

ACKNOWLEDGMENTS

I am convinced that the Benjamin Chee Chee's story needs to be told. The quality of his life and the manner of his death offer striking examples of the mindset of young Canadian Natives as well as an opportunity to comprehend the high incidence of suicides among this group. Canadians need to know about Benjamin Chee Chee, who he was, how he lived, and how he died, for his story is not unlike that of the thousands of other young Natives who have died by their own hand.

The message of the disastrous Chee Chee saga kept nudging me and demanding to be told, even though I had persuaded myself I was not the person to write the story because I was not Native. I had gone through the process of trying to contact Native leaders with the intent of receiving their blessing and encouragement. I did receive some encouragement, but it did not include the approbation for which I was searching. Finally, an old friend and colleague, Flora Peche, a Cree Native social worker who counsels Natives in the province of Alberta, gave me the name of a Dr Colin De'Ath, a former University of Waterloo colleague, who might know the whereabouts of Chee Chee's mother. I wrote to him at once. At the time he was working in Bangkok. He soon responded and gave me the name, address, and telephone number of

Frederick C. Brown in Victoria, B.C., suggesting that Brown could lead me to Josephine, Chee Chee's mother. With that connection everything began to fall into place. Brown put me in touch with Josephine, and we met at her home in Vancouver. She immediately understood what I intended and gave me the blessing I needed. Following that memorable meeting, the shape of the message that needed to be conveyed to the Canadian people began to form in my mind, and in a sense the book wrote itself.

The book was written in Finland. For many years I have summered in that beautiful country. Initially I went there to attend a congress of the International Association for Suicide Prevention and Crisis Intervention. Psychiatrist Dr John Ward and I were presenting papers on the suicide epidemic on the Wikwemikong Reserve on Manitoulin Island. I continued to return to Finland each summer to teach at one of their universities, research, lead workshops, and write. Among other things, I completed a major research project on the Finnish war children, which was published in Finnish. I also assisted with a couple of research projects for the Vasa chapter of the Finnish Cancer Society. I continued to be welcomed by the director and staff of the Cancer Society, which is a treatment clinic as well as having an educational function. Office space, computer equipment, and close relationships with the staff offer me a splendid environment for writing and contemplation. I want to thank the director, Teuvo Roden, and the members of his staff, particularly Gunnar Norrlund, Marita Uitto, and Esterita Tauriala, for their help and encouragement.

Many of my friends in Vasa belong to the medical and professional caregiving community. I particularly want to acknowledge the assistance of Dr Vivi-Ann Myllyniemi, a specialist in internal medicine at the Central Sjukhuset in Vasa, for her willingness to share medical knowledge and insights. Dr Helga Mills, the principal of St Paul's United College, a federated college of the University of Waterloo, has been an important resource person particularly with reference to the structure of the book. Dr Graham Brown, principal of St Paul's United College, University of Waterloo, has been supportive in many ways, ensuring the publication of the book. Dean James Gollnick and members of the faculty and staff of the college have always been willing to assist, especially Arlene Sleno and Dr Peter Frick for computer assistance. I am also grateful to Dr Robert Needham, the former director of the Canadian Studies Department at the college, and his Native Studies program staff.

The development of chapter 3, "Chee Chee the Artist," needed the guiding hand of a professional artist. I had the great good fortune to meet Fritz Jakobsson, a celebrated Finnish portrait painter, who willingly offered his artistic experience and knowledge in the several discussions I had with him. Members of "O" Division, Royal Canadian Mounted Police Veterans Association, shared experiences with me regarding investigations of suicide of Native people they had conducted while on active service. The British Broadcasting Corporation opened their archives with reference to the *Exxon Valdez* oil disaster off Alaska in 1989, the oil spill from the *Diamond Grace* that threatened Tokyo Bay in 1997, and the comments of Dr Robert Clarke, a marine biologist at Aberdeen University, Scotland. That material is used in the introduction of chapter 9, "The Healing." The BBC's immediate response is much appreciated.

Throughout the writing of the book I had the opportunity to speak with people who were friends of Benjamin Chee Chee. These include Norm Socha and Erla Boyer, owners of art galleries in Waterloo and Stratford, Ontario. Norm and Erla recognized Benjamin's artistic ability in the very early days of his emergence as an artist and promoted his work. Ernie Bies of the Department of Indian Affairs and Frederick C. Brown both had close relations with Benjamin. Despite the fact that they are white men, they probably were the closest and most consistent relationships Benjamin had. They were unstinting in the time they gave me in sharing information, feelings, and attitudes about the life and times of Benjamin Chee Chee as well as newspaper clippings, personal pictures, and other records. Their continued affection and enthusiasm for Benjamin has not died. They still mourn his death.

I had a memorable experience when, with some trepidation, I drove across the ice of Lake Temagami on a beautiful February day in 1998 to meet with Hugh McKenzie, a well-known Ojibway artist. Hugh and Benjamin grew up together on Bear Island. Ernie Bies told me that Benjamin thought of Hugh as a brother. When Benjamin had become established in Ottawa, he sent for Hugh and they painted together. Hugh and I spent a fine day in his home on Bear Island talking about Benjamin, his strengths and his frailties, and what it was like to be his friend. We spent time examining Hugh's art, and later he played his guitar and sang for me. Then he sent me for a walk around the island while he prepared a fish dinner for us. It was a wonderful day spent with a gracious, gentle, superb Native artist. I now have one of Hugh's fine paintings of a beautiful blue jay hanging in my living room.

I regret that my friend and colleague, the late Dr John Ward, was not available for consultation as I wrote the book. The research data of the Wikwemikong suicide epidemic described in chapter 6, "The Act of Suicide," was gathered by John and his associates and shared with me as we prepared our conference presentations in Helsinki in 1977.

The publication of the report of the Royal Commission on the Aboriginal Peoples could not have been more timely. I have not only read those volumes; I have carefully studied them. They are substantial, and I suspect that not many Canadians will undertake to read them. For those who want to understand the concerns of Canadian Natives, the commissioners' reports are a treasure-trove of information. Jean Becker, Aboriginal counsellor at St Paul's United College, University of Waterloo, has assisted me in working through that rich material.

The staff at the McMichael Canadian Art Collection have been very helpful in supplying reproductions of Chee Chee's art as well as advice in obtaining permission to publish this material. Also I extend my gratitude to Guy A. Mattar, administrator of the estate of Benjamin Chee Chee, for his immediate consent to use the artist's work in this book. The *Vancouver Sun* was generous in allowing me to use part of Wayne Edmonstone's fine article, "The Dying of Chee Chee."

Joan Harcourt, an editor at McGill-Queen's University Press, has been an enthusiastic supporter and guide throughout the saga of the birthing of this book. At times when it seemed likely it would not survive the passage to publication, Joan was there refusing to accept the verdict. I have felt her supportive presence beyond telling. Carol van Dyk and Andrée Gerard were willing readers examining each word and letter, striving for correction and authenticity. I have appreciated the thoroughness, sense of humour, and genuine warm humanness of the book's copy-editor, Maureen Garvie.

I am particularly grateful to the Nishnawbe Aski Nation for accepting my request and supplying me with a copy of the final report of the Nishnawbe Aski Nation Youth Forum on Suicide, *Horizons of Hope, An Empowering Journey*. I was a stranger to them, yet after a brief introduction through e-mail, their representatives accepted me and trusted me to use the information in the report in a responsible manner. It is a staggering four-hundred page message written by young people on the problem of suicide that has ravaged their nation. The report is the central source of chapter 8 of this book.

My wife, Barbara, has always been my most important ally, with her excellent eye and ear for the composition and the sound of words. Knowing when something has been well put together, she has not hesitated to tell me when it is out of tune. With her psychological, professional social-work background, including significant clinical experience, and a fine innate ability to understand others in depth, she has been an important resource in all of my writing and research efforts. For fifty years she has been the greatest of friends. Sadly, Barbara died before the publication of the book.

INTRODUCTION

In this book about aboriginal suicide I am speaking principally to the members of the white culture in Canadian society about our relationship with the First Nations people. I want white Canadians to know what our actions, attitudes, and feelings have done to the First Nations people in a specific way. That is, intentionally or non-intentionally, we have negatively affected Native people to the point that many, particularly the young, have opted to die rather than to live and be a part of Canadian society.

I hope members of the aboriginal people will also read this book. I feel it will convey to them that I and thousands of Canadians like me do struggle to fully appreciate the pain that Native people experience as the result of living among us. And we want that to stop!

I also want to be clear about who I am and my authority to write about this condition. I am not an expert in Native studies, though I consider myself well informed through my reading, studies, and contact with the Native people. In a course I taught on "Life Styles and Self-Destructive Behaviour" at the University of Waterloo, at the point where our study focused on aboriginal suicide, members of the Native population were invited into the classroom to present to the students. In a distance-education course on "Aging As Spiritual Journey," a former student of St Paul's who was born and presently lives on a Native reserve in Alberta shares a tape recording which has been heard by students across Canada and abroad, about his experience of life on a reserve.

I am an expert in suicide. I have completed significant research in the field of self-destructive behaviour and written papers which I have presented in many countries as a Lifetime Member of the International Association for Suicide Prevention and Crisis Intervention. As I noted, I have taught university-level courses on the subject of suicide. For nearly twenty-five years I have worked in university counselling services, mainly with depressed and suicidal students. I have a doctorate in psychology and clinical studies and have completed 30,000 hours of one-to-one psychotherapy, and many hundreds of hours of group psychotherapy. I am a registered marriage and family therapist. As a former member of the Royal Canadian Mounted Police, I have been involved in the investigation of a number of cases of suicide and homicide.

Recently I listened to a lecture presented by a Native speaker, a university professor who is a well-known author. She cautioned about members of the white race writing books about the life and times of aboriginal people. Her words impressed and helped me. In the process of completing and revising the manuscript for this book I received an important insight. It came to me that in this book about the high incidence of suicide among young Natives, I am not a white man describing the dynamics of Native culture. I am a member of the white culture writing about his own culture and how, consciously or unconsciously, we have abused First Nations people and led our children to develop abusive attitudes towards them. One of the glaring consequences of the stress of living with us is that many Native people, especially the young ones pondering their future, have concluded that they no longer can bear to live on those terms. Some prefer death.

This is a book about the suicide of the young. The suicide rate of young Canadian aboriginal men and women is among the highest in the world. White Canadians have played a key role in that terrible destruction. We need to understand those dynamics so we may be involved in the healing process, or at least not to hinder the recovery.

What follows is a summary of the book's organization. Chapter 1 describes three watershed experiences that led to my undertaking this project. In chapter 2, I describe Chee Chee's life, which ends in a suicide attempt in an Ottawa City Jail police cell. He sustained critical injuries that led to his death two days later in the Ottawa General Hospital. Chapter 3 focuses on Benjamin Chee Chee as an artist. The chapter includes his own understanding of his artistry, critics' views on his ability and promise, and a discussion of his final creation, the Black Geese Portfolio, which was delivered to his agent just hours before he attempted to kill himself. In chapter 4 I discuss Chee Chee's inheritance as an Ojibway revealing the positive elements of his birthright. Chapter 5 is a lengthy appraisal of the negative attitudes that twisted his personality and stunted his maturity. That was his inheritance as a Canadian Native.

This disturbing material opens the way to a detailed analysis in chapter 6 of the act of suicide and in particular the suicidal epidemic among young Natives. Chapter 7 focuses on the suicide of Benjamin Chee Chee and the issue of why he would end his own life at the time he was enjoying such success and recognition. Chapter 8 introduces the work of the Nishnawbe Aski Youth Forum on Suicide. The final report, *Horizons of Hope, an Empowering Journey*, reveals that culture has been devastated by the act of suicide. Chapter 9 offers a ray of hope and signs of healing. Although this examination of Chee Chee's life is a study in microcosm of ongoing self-destruction among Native people, it is vital to recognize that important change is underway. There is a feeling, though faint, of healing among Native people. If these early signs of recovery and healing are to continue to grow, then it is necessary for Native people to comprehend what is happening and to know how to respond.

Chapter 10, "Final Words," Benjamin Chee Chee again becomes the central focus. An event after his death and burial is brought to light, a symbolic happening that graphically highlights the problematic saga of a young man caught in the neurotic bind of a compelling need for love and approval, yet unable to accept them when they were offered.

CHEE CHEE

1

THE VIGIL

Three watershed experiences changed the flow of my life and led to the writing of this book. The first happened when I was twenty years old and a member of the Royal Canadian Mounted Police. Following basic training, my first posting was to the Rose Valley RCMP detachment in central Saskatchewan. A message had been received from the Indian agent of the nearby Nut Lake Indian Reserve that a Native woman had been found dead in the forest. An investigation was requested, suggesting that the death was something other than natural or accidental.

There were two RCMP officers stationed at Rose Valley. The senior officer was Steve, a veteran of twelve years in the force; I was the other. I had about two and a half years of experience as a cadet with a municipal police department before my posting to Rose Valley. The Nut Lake Reserve was the home of a large group of Cree Natives, who lived quietly among themselves surviving mainly by fishing and hunting. A few members of the band worked on neighbouring farms during the harvest season.

Soon after I arrived at Rose Valley, I sensed an unmistakable division between the townspeople and the Native community. This feeling was not expressed in an aggressive or arrogant manner. The town itself was the home of about five hundred men, women, and children. It was made up of a few grain elevators, a railway station, half a dozen stores, an elementary and secondary school, a small hotel, and a doctor's office. The townspeople were friendly and hospitable. It was a gentle, peaceful, kindly environment.

The town was quite separate from the Indian reserve. Natives were seldom seen in the community. The townspeople, though not belligerent in their attitude, had the feeling that the Natives were strange, unstable, unpredictable, and inferior to themselves. Though it was understood that most of the Natives could speak and understand English, generally they refused to communicate other than in their Native tongue. It was clearly an expression of their resentment towards a people who refused to treat them as equals.

In the brief period I was stationed at the Rose Valley detachment, I did not meet anyone in the town who actually knew anything about the Natives. They did not know who they were, how long they had lived there, where they were from, or why they were there. Nor, in my work on the reserve, did I meet any Native who expressed any interest in the town and its community, and this included the Indian agent. The Native community and the town community existed as two solitudes, though they obviously had feelings about each other.

Some of the townspeople felt that the Natives were dangerous. This feeling was somewhat justified, for on occasion some Native men would become violent when they consumed bootleg liquor supplied by distillers who had set up their stills near the reserve. In those days Natives were not allowed to buy legal alcoholic beverages. In their drunken condition some became enraged and acted out powerful feelings related to being ignored and despised.

I had been in Rose Valley only a few short months prior to the mysterious death on the reserve. Convinced by the stories of the townspeople and also by accounts from RCMP officers in neighbouring detachments about aggressive and dangerous Natives, I was apprehensive as we set out to investigate. We followed the Indian agent to a clearing in the forest, where we found the body of a young Native woman about my age. We estimated that she had been dead for two days. She was lying on her back, her feet bare, her moccasins placed together at the side of her body. Across her chest was a single shot, .22 calibre Cooey rifle. The gun was old and rusty, but it functioned. A discharged shell was still in the chamber. She had a small gunshot wound in her chest and there was a large hole in her back where the projectile had exited. Powder burns on her moose-hide tunic indicated that the gun had been discharged at very close range.

Apparently she had killed herself. Attempting to reconstruct the event, we conjectured that after removing her moccasins she lay on her back and held the old rifle by the end of the barrel ready and cocked for firing. She aimed the muzzle at her heart and discharged the gun by pressing her toe against the trigger. This scenario was conjecture and not a certainty. Since homicide was still a possibility, the presence of a coroner, a medical doctor appointed by the province to investigate questionable deaths, was required. He would conduct his own investigation as well as assist us in our work. He would also arrange for the post-mortem examination and possibly require that an inquest court be convened.

In those days in that part of the world we did not have police-car radios, and telephones were not easily available. Someone needed to return to the Rose Valley police detachment and bring the coroner back to the death scene. In northern Canada in mid-October, darkness closes in early. My partner, the senior man at the detachment, could have ordered me to stand guard and returned to Rose Valley to make arrangements. But we did not operate that way. Regardless of seniority, we were partners who trusted each other and worked on a consensus basis. I urged Steve to return to town and spend the evening with his wife, Ella. I suspect that he heard a lack of enthusiasm in my voice. He said that we would decide on the flip of a coin. We did, and I lost.

After Steve and the Indian agent departed, I felt anxious and alone. In my early teens I had read most of the adventure books in my hometown public library. Many stories portrayed Native people as silent aggressors stalking their prey, especially at night. The message had stayed with me. It was now pitch dark. An undulating ghostlike noise caused by the wind moaning through the pines and the dry leaves still left on the birches deepened my unease. The moon broke briefly through the cloud cover, then disappeared again.

I stayed close to the body for I found being alone in such a situation nerve-wracking. Suddenly a projectile careened through the air, smashed against my Stetson hat, knocked it off my head, and sent it flying! I drew my service revolver, ready for an attack. None came. I recovered my hat some ten feet away and found it dented on one side. I wondered later if a bird had struck it. It was all very strange and upsetting.

Whatever it was, the incident broke the tension. My anxiety began to lessen, and I felt increasingly calm and "on duty." I paced up and down but did not go far from the body. I was there to look after her, to protect any evidence of what might have been a homicide. I felt a strong sense of purpose. I was there to see that the young woman's body was not disturbed by animals or anything else.

The night wore slowly on but no longer seemed interminable. As the clouds rolled away, the moon shone brightly. At about two A.M. I heard the noise of several persons tramping through the brush. This time I did not feel the need to draw my revolver. Whoever was out there wanted to be certain they were heard. I quietly waited. Into the clearing, in single file, walked five Native men. They did not speak. There was not a word or sign of greeting or explanation.

When they reached the point where I stood by the body, they stopped. In precision they squatted on the ground in a semi-circle. There we were – the dead Native girl, five Native men, and myself. The scene was lit by the full moon, the only sound the wind moaning gently through the leaves.

I felt deeply calm. I began to realize that they were there for the same reason I was. We were keeping vigil. While their motivation was different, our purpose was the same. We were there to watch over her. Though they did not intend it, they were also meeting my needs. I was no longer alone. I was grateful for their companionship.

While I felt compelled to express my gratitude and welcome, the only gifts I had were cigarettes. Steve and the Indian agent had both given me their supply before they left. I have long since given up smoking, but on that occasion I was glad I had something to share. I offered them my cigarettes, not realizing until years later the symbolic meaning of offering the gift of tobacco to Aboriginal people. They did not view it as a symbolic offering, nor did I intend it as such. They accepted my gift, and we lit up. We did not speak to each other that entire night, not one word; it was indeed a silent vigil. I distributed cigarettes until my supply ran out.

Slowly the eastern sky started to brighten. As if by some pre-arranged signal my companions stood up and, walking in single file, disappeared into the forest. This time I did not hear the tramping feet or the rustling of fallen leaves as they simply faded silently into the brush.

Steve returned with the coroner and the Indian agent,

bearing gifts from Ella of hot coffee, muffins, and fruit. The coroner concurred with our summary investigation that the death was indeed a suicide. Later the results of a post-mortem examination established the probable motive of her self-destruction. The young Native woman was pregnant and unmarried. The coroner was of the opinion that this desperate situation had driven her to take her life.

Something of a profound nature happened to me that night long ago when the Natives and I kept vigil. Though unspoken, a kinship had developed. We had not reached the spiritual depth of the peace pipe ritual as we smoked together, but their willingness to receive my gift and smoke with me expressed our mutual recognition and acceptance of one another. Their vigil was allied to their spiritual beliefs, mine to a pragmatic one. Yet the essence of vigil is watchfulness and caring, and that is precisely why we were there. With the coming of the light, the evil spirits of the night no longer threatened.

I have never forgotten the experiences of that night. For me, it was the beginning of the development of a more enlightened attitude toward Native people. Through the process of knowledge and understanding, and the development of close relationships with Native people, some of whom were my students and others friends, associates, and colleagues, a sense of respect and kinship continued to grow. The vigil was a turning point in my life. I began to establish a foundation that would be the basis of important decisions and actions that I hope will be the means of relieving some of the pain and suffering so evident in the lives of Native people. These activities were involved in my profession as professor, psychologist, suicidologist, and writer.

The second watershed event occurred in June 1977 when I was preparing to travel to Helsinki, Finland, to attend a Congress of the International Association of Suicide Prevention and Crisis Intervention. John Ward and I were presenting papers on the subject of Native suicide in Canada. John, a psychiatrist, and Joseph Fox, a Native counsellor, had prepared a paper for the congress on the suicide epidemic that occurred on the Wikwemikong Reserve on Manitoulin Island in Northern Ontario in 1976. My paper was a background study related to the issues of culture, identity loss, and other significant factors that had led to numerous suicides among Native people.

These papers were the first major studies to be presented to an international scientific body on the high incidence of suicide among Natives in Canada. Following my presentation the chairperson called for questions or responses. I felt privileged that Dr Edwin S. Shneidman, one of the world's most renowned suicidologists, was present. Among his other comments he said: "It seems that Canadians don't like their Natives very much."

Just before I left for Helsinki to present that paper, my wife, Barbara, had told me that some of the remaining works of Benjamin Chee Chee were being sold at the Inukshuk Gallery in Waterloo, Ontario. Barbara had bought two of Chee Chee's original works in 1976 from the gallery. We both enjoyed them, and I still do. The sale was an opportunity to add to our collection. Barbara told me the sad news that Chee Chee had committed suicide a few months earlier.

When we arrived at the gallery, the sale had not yet begun. A noisy throng of people jammed the small space, anxious to buy a Chee Chee. Norm and Erla Socha, the gallery owners, drew me aside. Early in Chee Chee's career they had recognized him as an artist in the field of Canadian Native art who was breaking new ground. They had always been advocates and supporters of Native art, and they were devastated and deeply saddened at the news of his death. For Norm and Erla the sale of his works was not just an ordinary sale: it marked the end of Benjamin Chee Chee and his artistic creations.

They were bothered by the clamour and the motive of financial gain that had brought many people to the gallery that night. They felt that those who had come to the sale needed to know about Chee Chee, his background, and the forces that had led him to destroy himself. They invited me to open the sale with a statement, which I was pleased to do so.

The group became quiet and listened intently as I talked about the saga of Aboriginal people in Canada and their deterioration as a people when they became overwhelmed by their experiences with the white race. Briefly I tried to explain how Native people had experienced the loss of their culture, heritage, status, identity, and meaning in life. The consequence of these losses had introduced feelings of despair that led some to drug abuse, alcoholism, and suicide. I described Chee Chee's family background, personality, lifestyle, and history as typical of many young Natives who had committed suicide. I shared my feeling that there were no quick and easy answers that would add hope to the Natives' awful dilemma. I ended by adding that I expected that many other young Natives would follow in Chee Chee's way. Regretfully, many have done so.

Since then I have wanted to tell Chee Chee's whole story. I feel that the drama of his life and death is the expression of the existential hopelessness and meaninglessness that many young Natives experience in Canada. There are many Benjamin Chee Chees among the million Natives who inhabit Canada. They are fine young men and women, rich in talent, yet filled with despair that directs them to end a life that offers no hope of change.

As I have noted in my acknowledgments, I was reluctant to write Chee Chee's story. I have hesitated to do so not because

I lack the qualifications. My hesitation is related to the culture in which I was born, and to which I belong. I am a white Anglo-Saxon. The white race played a significant role in Chee Chee's death and continues to be involved in the ongoing trauma of Native people. For those reasons I was convinced that it was improper for a white person to tell Chee Chee's story. I believe that for too long non-Aboriginal persons have written, created policies, and taken action regarding a culture that is not their own. The time has come for Natives to speak for themselves. It is starting to happen.

Eventually I was encouraged to write this book by Native people, but I felt I needed the approval, and the blessing, from Chee Chee's own family. The third watershed happening occurred when I received that approval. In March 1996 I finally located Josephine Roy, Benjamin Chee Chee's mother, in Vancouver. It was a great pleasure and privilege to meet with this woman. Unfortunately she died in the fall of 1997 before the publication of the book.

When we met in Vancouver I came bearing two gifts: maple sugar, from her home province of Quebec, and sweet grass, a gift from the Grand River Mohawks. During our visit she supported and approved of my intent to tell Benjamin Chee Chee's story. Josephine shared information with me about her life with her son. She also loaned me snapshots of him at work in his studio. We continued to correspond until her death.

2

CHEE CHEE: A LIFE

My name is Benjamin and I have a problem!
  —Benjamin Chee Chee

At a party in Montreal in 1969 Benjamin Chee Chee introduced himself to Frederick C. Brown, a lawyer, with the following words: "My name is Benjamin and I have a problem."
The line came from the film *The Graduate*, starring Dustin
Hoffman. Chee Chee thought the words pertinent to his
own life situation, and it became his method of introducing
himself.

It is unlikely that he ever realized the depth and intensity
of his ultimate problem. He does not appear to have been a
reflective person. Missing was the ability to raise to conscious comprehension the pervading presence of a violent
nature and the inner destructiveness that would eventually
kill him. But even with awareness and understanding of his
own psyche it is unlikely that he could have averted the
tragedy to follow. His life was on a self-destructive trajecto-
ry from the beginning.

He was born on 26 March 1944, in the northern Ontario
town of Temagami in the home of Angele, the first wife of
British-born Archie Belaney, who became famous as the
"Indian" naturalist Grey Owl. The young parents named the

baby Kenneth Thomas Chee Chee, and Angele added the name Benjamin. He was raised on the Indian reserve of Bear Island on Lake Temagami. He would die on 11 March 1977 in the Ottawa General Hospital from the effects of a suicide attempt in an Ottawa police cell, a few days short of his thirty-third birthday. From the time of his birth to the hour of his death, his life has been described as a "wild ride."[1]

His father, Angus Chee Chee, an Ojibway Native, worked as a guide for a tourist resort. Benjamin's mother, Josephine, an Algonquin Native, was employed as a housekeeper at the same resort. Angus and Josephine fell in love and married. Benjamin was their only child. In the first winter of Benjamin's life, while Angus was gathering firewood along the shore of Lake Temagami, the truck he was driving crashed through the ice. Two companions leaped to safety, but Angus was trapped in the truck and was drowned. Benjamin was without a father.

Father, father where are you going?
   Oh, do not walk so fast!
Speak, father, speak to your little boy,
   Or else I shall be lost.[2]

Angus's body was recovered, and he was buried on Bear Island on Benjamin's first birthday. It was a prophetic sign of the painful saga that lay ahead. Though the connection with the mother continues to be a vital link throughout the child's life, social science research reveals that at a very early age the relationship with the father is vital for the continued development and well-being of children of both genders. From the father the male child receives his masculine identity, just as the female child is aided by the father's presence in the development of her femaleness.

Benjamin was soon also to lose his mother. Emotionally the bond was broken with her in his early years. Josephine had never attended school and had always worked as a cleaner. After Angus's death she had to leave Benjamin alone or with friends while she went out to search for work. The small widow's allowance of $30 a month was not enough to pay for food and lodging. She was not available to offer a mother's care and presence when Benjamin needed her. By the time he was twelve he had lost her forever, with the exception of a few months at the end of his life. Even then they remained strangers. Peter Allard, the marketing manager of the Fine Art Department of the Canadian Indian Marketing Services, once observed, "I think a lot of what he did and wanted to accomplish in the years before he found his mother were motivated by his search for her and his not finding her. I suspect he was disappointed when he did find her."[3]

Anticipation or expectation seldom live up to reality. Josephine told me, "I don't know my own son. He was taken away from me when he was twelve years old. We never got back together again."

From the beginning of his life Chee Chee was alone, without parents and family. He was to make his way through life as an isolate, yearning for closeness but never experiencing it. Some of his art graphically underlines that fact. Learning early that closeness causes pain, rejection follows intimacy, he lacked the will and the capacity to sustain long-term relationships. He had developed the protective wisdom that to live safely is to live at arms' length.

He was a person of fine stature, a tall handsome man with strong Native features. His thick, black hair hung past his shoulders. He is described as often wearing a disarming, boyish grin on his face. His public persona was extraverted and outgoing, a style not to be mistaken for openness and an abil-

ity to relate intimately. Driving him was an apparently inex-
haustible reservoir of emotional energy. Lacking was purpose
or direction in the expression of that dynamic energy. He was
often lost, confused, uncertain, simply drifting wherever the
current would carry him. His life was a roller-coaster ride,
sometimes wild, sometimes calmer, and always unpredictable.

Early in life he found a substance that temporarily replaced
feelings of fear and turmoil with feelings of confidence and
inner peace. It gave him what human relationships had failed
to offer. The substance was alcohol. Both his parents and
many friends and relatives on the reserve had made the same
discovery.

He spent almost a third of his brief life in penal institutions
including time served in the infamous Bordeaux Quebec
prison for charges related to fighting with the police.[4] His
offences were not of an indictable criminal nature; mainly
they were for being drunk and disorderly. If he broke any
other laws, alcohol was the trigger. He was not malicious or
vindictive. Under the right circumstances, in a positive, secure
environment, he showed a caring, and generous spirit. Often
he was like a sick, confused child. His unfortunate beginnings
were to contaminate his life and bring about its end.

At the age of twelve, categorized as a juvenile delinquent,
he was despatched to Alfred, an industrial training school
operated by the Christian Brothers. Discharged, he wandered
home. He did not get along with Josephine's new husband
and soon became a drifter. He was searching for something
that he could grasp, some hold on life that would prevent him
from sinking into oblivion.

He found that something in the world of art. For the final
few years of his life art absorbed him, gave him direction. Art
uncovered within his psyche a creative genius, the manifestation of which would deeply touch the lives of many. For a

brief time his being was able to cling to a life-giving resource. However, his grip on it was tenuous. The forces allied against him were too powerful.

As a child Chee Chee had demonstrated an interest in art. It was Frederick Brown, the lawyer he had met at the party in Montreal, who found him a place in the artistic world. Without Brown there would have been no Benjamin Chee Chee, the artist. Though he would balk at being so described, Brown was Chee Chee's "necessary angel."

Brown understood Chee Chee at a deeper level than any person I have met. Well groomed, urbane, more young than old, he has an impressive stature and appears very fit. He is direct, confident, and approachable. As a lieutenant colonel in the Canadian Army, Brown served overseas in World War II. A graduate of McMaster University and Osgoode Hall, he successfully practised law in Hamilton for thirteen years, then pursued other interests, generally connected with the law. He lived and worked in Montreal, Ottawa, Regina, and, ultimately, in Victoria, B.C., served with federal and provincial Royal Commissions, and in the last twenty-one years has engaged in juridical writing for publications.

Brown is a care-giver, but he is extremely selective in his care-giving. Those he selects find his help unstinting and unconditional. He is wise in the nature of what he is prepared to give and has an ingrained instinct of when to be present and when to be absent. With an incisive, analytical mind, he quickly comprehends and appraises a situation and the environment surrounding it. It is not surprising that his work now involves distilling legal judgments from the supreme courts, reducing them to a language that practising lawyers can understand and use without losing the essence of the judge's decision.

Soon after their meeting, Brown realized that Chee Chee

needed someone who could befriend him unconditionally, someone who was prepared to take on the role of surrogate father. Brown decided he would take on that task. Because Chee Chee also needed someone with the experience and the wisdom to introduce him to the world of art, Brown introduced him to a prominent Montreal artist, Dorothy Watt.

It was precisely the right referral. On numerous occasions Chee Chee publicly recognized Dorothy as the person who had the greatest artistic influence on his life. She was able to stimulate and encourage his interest in art and be his mentor. Chee Chee gave full credit to her for being the person instrumental in his pursuing art as a career.

Dorothy and her husband, Robin Watt, renowned portrait artists, had spent most of their professional lives in England painting famous people including royalty. "I introduced Benny to her and she took to him immediately," Brown told me. "She could see that he had talent." Dorothy was associated with the Canadian Guild of Crafts in Montreal, where she found a place for Chee Chee. This connection opened the way for him to meet with other artists in Montreal. With Dorothy's help he was finding his way into the art world. He was deeply pleased and excited by this turn of events.

Though the guild could not pay him for his work in displaying the guild's art and artifacts, Dorothy gave him art lessons and found a place for him to work in her studio. This arrangement worked out very well for him. Recognizing his progress, Dorothy gave him a set of brushes, palettes, and paints and a wooden chest to contain all his new equipment. Chee Chee treasured these gifts and used them throughout his career.

"That got him working on his art, and then in order to eat I was able to get him a job as a warehouseman for a business whose owner I knew. He did an excellent job there," Brown recalled. One of Chee Chee's jobs at the warehouse was to drive his employer's Cadillac convertible downtown to the service station to get the car washed and filled with gasoline and the oil checked. Brown comments: "On at least three different occasions he was stopped by the police just because he was an Indian driving an expensive car. And he never did anything wrong. So you can see how Benny at that point, though I think he had similar experiences earlier in his life, was developing a hatred for the police, because they did harass him."

Yet life had taken an upward turn for Benjamin Chee Chee. His aspiration to be an artist was becoming real. He was working and had money. He met a lovely young French-Canadian woman, Lucille L'Orange. Brown described her as "a very nice person, a little wee girl. Benny used to pick her up and throw her around like a doll, which she loved." Brown felt that the relationship was good for both of them. But, he added "She couldn't stop him from drinking."

Brown said that on occasion when Chee Chee was drinking he would exhibit a "consuming hatred." I commented that "hatred" was a strong word. He responded: "I know it is a strong word. I use it advisedly. When Benny was at a certain point of intoxication, you could just see the hatred in his eyes, and you would almost think that he was ready to kill you just because you were white!" I responded: "Just because you were white? It is interesting that he was still able to relate to you, and continued to do so." Brown replied: "He loved me, there was no question of that. I was sort of a father figure, I think. He depended upon me, I never treated him badly. I always treated him as an equal, which of course he was. I was kind to his little girl. In fact they lived with me for a little while. I took them in and they stayed in my spare bedroom. They were fine people to have there."

In 1972, when they became more established, Lucille and Chee Chee moved to the east end of Montreal into a small apartment. There he set up his own studio and began to produce some of his early paintings. To survive he found a job painting a building which had been used in Expo 67. For at least two years they remained there. Chee Chee worked experimentally and produced new art forms. He kept in contact with Dorothy Watt, who continued to be his friend, teacher, and mentor. He worked at a variety of menial jobs for a living.

Although Chee Chee trusted Dorothy Watt and Brown, his general distrust of white people remained. Brown felt that this was an inheritance from the past, sustained by experiences Chee Chee had with white people from time to time: "If he was drinking in a bar, he would be perfectly fine until a waiter or bartender gave him a hard time. Then he would become nasty. Otherwise he wouldn't. He just didn't get mad for no reason at all. But he would work himself up to a rage, and you could see him doing it. It was a terrifying thing to watch because you knew it would end in some kind of an explosion, and you would hope that you would not be in the middle of it."

When drunk, he could be extremely violent. One of his drinking partners said: "Outwardly he had great confidence in himself and his work. But when he was drinking, there seemed to be a persecution complex there ... he would get mean, vulgar, and sometimes violent." Brown commented: "In my opinion any time the police beat Benny, he asked for it. And he never complained. He was not a victim." When the police came to apprehend him for drunkenness and disturbing the peace, he was not inclined to go quietly. Brown witnessed two policemen trying to arrest him for being drunk and disorderly in Montreal. Soon the officers were joined by three others. Brown reports that in the fight Chee Chee knocked down the five police officers. By the time he was taken into custody, approximately ten officers were involved in making the arrest.

Josephine also told me that he would come home, his clothes torn and dirty, and tell stories of how the police assaulted him. On one occasion he told her that five policemen tied him up and beat him.

In 1972 Brown moved to Ottawa to take the position of administrative assistant to Gerald LeDain, chairman of the federal Commission of Inquiry into the Non-Medical Use of Drugs. Brown did not forget Chee Chee who had just gone through a demoralizing experience. Someone had arranged an exhibition of his work, which had not gone well. "Everyone had scoffed at his work. The Quebecois pseudo-intelligentsia derided his art because he had never studied at L'Ecole des Beaux Arts: 'How could he possibly be a painter!' It put him down badly."

Immediately Brown set to work. He knew that he was dealing with a talented individual who was also very fragile and could easily be destroyed. He turned to the Department of Indian Affairs and was referred to Kathy Everts at the department's Cultural Development and Education Branch. Brown can be very convincing, and he was able to persuade Everts to visit Chee Chee in Montreal and view his work. She was so impressed that she immediately bought ten pieces at $150 each. Brown said: "She saw the talent." He added, "Benny went right through the roof!"

Brown urged Chee Chee to move to Ottawa, persuading him that there was no future for him in the Montreal art world. He and Lucille moved to Ottawa, and Brown found Lucille a job as telephone receptionist with the LeDain Commission. He also began to explore possibilities that would lead

to an exhibition of Chee Chee's works. He introduced him
to Pierre and Marie Gaignery, owners of the Nicholas Art
Gallery in Ottawa. Brown recalled Chee Chee's first exhibition
at the Nicholas Gallery in 1973. "He was so shy. You wouldn't
have known he was the artist. But it was well-attended, and it
was sold out. That was another boost for him."

The work of the LeDain Commission completed, Brown
left Ottawa to take up residence and work in Victoria, B.C. He
was not to see Chee Chee again until 1977, though Chee Chee
would frequently call him to talk – "often in the middle of the
night." Over those next years Chee Chee continued to produce new works. He became well known and the public
responded to his art.

In July 1976 he finally located his mother, after searching
for her for years. He received word that she was working on
an island with her niece and her husband at a tourist camp.
He immediately set out and brought Josephine to Ottawa.
Josephine describes the occasion: "He hired a plane and flew
in to get me. I was in the water swimming with the children,
and he walked right in and picked me up and carried me to
shore." Chee Chee was wearing a $400 suit at the time. I asked
Josephine if she enjoyed the time in Ottawa. "Oh yes, when he
was not drinking." "Was he drinking quite a lot?" I asked.
"Yes," she quietly replied.

By now Lucille had left Chee Chee and returned to
Montreal. Brown described the reason for their breakup: "He
became physically abusive. He wasn't [like that] in the early
stages. He was so kind to her. But this happened. I think it
happened because she never recognized his talent. She would
say: 'Oh, Benny, why don't you get a real job?' Little Yvette –
little bourgeois – her man is no good unless her man is going
to work every day and coming home at night to put bread on

the table. The fact that she couldn't understand that he was an artist rankled and annoyed Benny. Finally, when he lashed out at her, she had to leave. It became intolerable."

During that same period Chee Chee began to use drugs. "He sought new experiences and began to experiment with soft drugs," his friend Ernie Bies told me. "His philosophy became, 'live for today for you may not be here tomorrow.' A bad personal experience with LSD and being present when a friend died of a drug overdose frightened him sufficiently to confine his use to marijuana and mescaline."[5]

The next time Chee Chee and Brown met was in March 1977 in Brown's home in Victoria. At that time five exhibitions of Chee Chee's works were in process in Vancouver, Ottawa, Toronto, Halifax, and Winnipeg. Plans were being made for exhibitions in New York and Munich as well. Chee Chee's art was not well known in western Canada, but the first exhibition of his work in Vancouver immediately sold out. The gallery owner urgently requested more paintings, and Brown's home became an art studio. "Benny said sure," Brown recalled. "He did five more in one morning. We rushed them over to Vancouver. They framed them. He called them his Benny Birds. He said, 'I can do a Benny Bird in nothing flat.'"

When Brown had last seen him in 1973, Chee Chee was drinking socially, "but not as a drunkard." When they met in 1977 following the opening of the Vancouver exhibition, Brown said Chee Chee's drinking was out of control. "He was drinking much more heavily and much more extensively. At that point he drank only Chivas Regal scotch whisky. And in such copious quantities it would appal you."

During that visit Brown and Chee Chee sat up most of the night talking. "He talked and he talked and I don't even remember the things he said, but they were such distressful statements about his early life and what he thought of life. It was obviously coming from his soul and he was deeply, deeply disturbed. He wanted to tell someone and he figured he could tell me. He was terribly morose, not angry [but] sad." His outlook the next morning vividly demonstrated the mood swings that dominated him. The cloud had lifted. He told Brown: "I love this place. I'm going to bring my mother out and we are going to live here. Now it doesn't matter where I live. They know me and I can live here and I can enjoy the island, and the forest, and the sea." In a matter of days he would be dead.

He returned to Ottawa to complete the work he had promised to Peter Allard, the marketing manager of the Canadian Indian Marketing Service's Fine Art Department. On 11 March 1977 he delivered the eighteen paintings now known as the Black Geese Portfolio, a series highly praised by artist and curator Robert Houle. Chee Chee then went to Jimmy's Restaurant on Bank Street, a tavern he frequented. Police were called to find a window had been broken and Chee Chee "boisterous and intoxicated." He was placed under arrest and secured at 6.50 P.M. in police cell no. 10, "simply a cage with bars on all sides and no furniture at all"[6] reserved for uncooperative prisoners. Minutes later Chee Chee was found hanging from the bars of the cell. He had hung himself with a noose fashioned from his shirt. He died in hospital three days later.

The police were unable to get in touch with Josephine, who was in Toronto attending a meeting of Alcoholics Anonymous, but they found Brown's name and telephone number in Chee Chee's wallet. "He was alive and in the hospital when the police called," Brown said. "They gave me the number of the hospital and the name of the doctor. I called and he told me that he didn't expect Benjamin to live, that he was fighting to live, but the brain damage that had been done was so extensive that it probably wouldn't be a good idea if he did live. Later the doctor called me back and said, 'He's gone.'"

Brown did not attend the funeral or the inquest. Aboriginal people in Ottawa accorded Chee Chee full honours. He lay in state at the Indian Friendship Centre surrounded by many of his artistic works. The native community posted an honour guard. So did the Ottawa police. "Benny would have loved that," said Brown.

Many years after, Brown is still deeply angry over the death. He will carry those feelings to the grave. The emotions he expressed in a letter to the editor of the *Ottawa Citizen* shortly after Chee Chee's death can still be felt:

Please grant me the privilege of paying tribute to, and mourning the passing of a worthy man. Benjamin Chee Chee was an Ojibway artist of national renown, indeed the possibility of international fame was imminent. He, like most of us, had certain failings, the most prominent of which was his taste for alcohol. This, however, never interfered with the quality of his work or his steady production. Three recent exhibitions (Toronto, Vancouver, Winnipeg) all attest to this fact. On March 11, having lunched with his Mother, he delivered 20 paintings to his agent, being noted at the time as extremely well dressed and well-pleased with his efforts. A few hours later he was near death in the intensive care ward of Ottawa General Hospital; he had hanged himself in a cell at the Ottawa Police Station. Why was he there? He had, according to the official report, been arrested on a downtown street "in an intoxicated condition." Had he been a senator, a cabinet minister, a prominent businessman (and I am sure that some members of those august groups suffer from a similar affliction) he might have been driven home. After all, he lived at the Embassy Apartment Hotel – not too far out of the way from any downtown point. However, I suppose that "drunken" Indians must be treated as such.

Frederick C. Brown
Victoria, B.C.[7]

The remorse of lost hope also lingers on in Brown's mind: "If he had got back here, he might still be alive. I think that a whole new area of his career would have opened here. He was successful enough that he was making plenty of money, and I think if he had settled down I would have had an opportunity to have an influence on him. If he had been here I think I could have been a good influence. But the short time he was here, there was nothing I could do but put up with him."

The sudden, wilful act of self-destruction was tragic in the extreme. News of Chee Chee's death was reported by the media across the nation. His suicide was discussed and articles were published about the quality of his art and his artistic legacy. For those who watched his star in ascension, its crash was shocking. Many grieved. Some saw it as an opportunity and rushed to purchase what remained of his work as prices started to escalate. An art review by Nancy Baele, published in the *Ottawa Citizen* in May 1977 reported, "Prices have skyrocketed and a popular limited edition print, titled Scramble, sells at the present time for $9500."[8] Previously it had been sold for a few hundred dollars. Accusations followed the materialistic reaction. Chee Chee's suicide, one newspaper noted, "created a bonzana for art dealers while at the same moment native friends were trying to collect money to keep him from a pauper's grave."[9]

The RCMP were called in to investigate the Canadian Indian

Marketing Service, responding to complaints that some of Chee Chee's work might have been sold as damaged goods at less than their real value. Daniel Gaignery, son of Pierre and Marie Gaignery, who were responsible for opening the way for Chee Chee's art career, was appointed co-administrator of Chee Chee's estate. He soon had to hire a bodyguard after receiving anonymous telephone threats because "the white man is ripping off the Indians once again."[10] It was a period of grief, confusion, greed, anger, and uncertainty. Rudy Platiel noted in the *Globe and Mail*, "It is perhaps not surprising that controversy follows in the wake of an artist who lived his life in the same spirit as the wild, reckless, joy-riding car chases on which he led police as a young man."[11]

3

CHEE CHEE THE ARTIST

Art is a language in images by which man communicates his ideas, his conceptions of himself, his fellowmen, and his universe. —William Fleming, *Art, Music, and Ideas*[1]

Each year Dr Margaretha Ivars celebrates the arrival of the Finnish summer with a garden party at an elegant country site in central Finland. With care she selects and invites about twenty or thirty people whom she feels will find each other interesting companions. I have been invited to Margaretha's garden party a number of times. The fact that I am usually the only Canadian academic hovering around those parts is likely one reason for that privilege. At this year's party I had the good fortune to meet someone I had heard of but not met. "My name is Fritz Jakobsson," he said. "I'm an artist."

"My name is Al Evans," I replied. "I'm a professor who needs, at this very moment in life, to spend some time with an artist." I explained that I was writing a book about a Canadian Native artist, and I needed guidance in understanding the world of art.

Fritz Jakobsson is a celebrated Finnish portrait artist with over one hundred exhibitions of his work throughout Europe. Recently he completed a portrait of Queen Sylvia of Sweden and also a portrait of the Pope. Of equal importance,

for my purposes, he is a reflective person who can conceptu-
alize and communicate his inner experiences. I felt an immediate kinship with him, and he with me. We had a wonderful
and lengthy conversation. I tried to remember his every word.

Before I met Fritz, a friend had told me an anecdote about
him that revealed an interesting and significant part of his
personality. Fritz and his family had lived in a large, wooden
heritage house, a fine old structure where he had his studio.
A fire swept through the building, burning it to the ground.
No one was injured, but hundreds of Fritz's paintings were
destroyed. Following this catastrophe he walked downtown
and went into a tavern, sat alone, and drank a glass of beer
while he reflected upon his losses. He concluded that he had
really not lost anything, for everything he had created was still
deeply embedded in his memory. He left the tavern determined to build a new home and a new studio, and to continue with his artistic career. His response was also a typical
Finnish approach to life.

"Do you mind if I tell you what I mean by art?" he said,
cutting through a superficial small talk one makes in the early
stages of meeting someone new.

"Please do," I said. "I feel this is why we have been brought
together." Our meeting was a synchronistic event; the timing
could not have been more perfect.

"We are all artists," he began. I had both read and heard
that same statement years ago from several different sources,
initially from the work of sociologist Margaret Mead, who
wrote of our innate creativity. I have always felt a certainty
about that truth. Despite age, gender, race, creed, intellect, or
aptitude, we all have the potential to be creative, to express
ourselves in a variety of ways.

If, then, all humans are artists, what is the purpose of having such a gift? In Fritz's understanding of the meaning of art,

this question is vital. He is convinced that the central issue in life is to know yourself, a demanding task, and then on the basis of that knowledge to live a creative existence. He agrees with Plato's statement: "The unexamined life is not worth living." Fritz views art as a way of presenting ourselves for the purpose of personal discernment, a developing awareness that may lead to a deeper comprehension of the self, which could lead to a fuller life's experience. "Art is a projection of the self. No one can know or understand himself fully, but we must try." Fritz feels strongly that art is closely related to the issue of identity. He made that point a number of times. "We are forever struggling to know who we are. We put our art on the wall and then we look to see how others respond to it. We use our art as mirrors so we can view ourselves." As we stood on the verandah of Margaretha's house, Fritz walked over and framed a picture with his hands on the back wall. "See!"

Fritz used the term "identity" in a profound way. Identity, he explained, is connected with the entire meaning of existence. Identity, the search for the self, is basic to all of the existential issues related to the meaning of life: purpose, direction, meaning, birth, life, and death. The primary function of art is to be a resource that enables us to discover who we are, to comprehend more fully the incomprehensible, the human personality. So a child brings home a piece of art which he has created in the schoolroom and presents it to his parents, anxious to see their response. He wants to know how they feel about it because he hungers for recognition and approval. All those issues, Fritz claimed, are related to the central fact of identity.

In recent times art therapy has become an important therapeutic process that can reveal even to the untrained eye what is going on in the inner person. One of my clients, a young woman in her mid-twenties studying fine art and theology, was referred to me because she was clinically depressed. She had an outstanding ability in clay sculpturing. I was able to help her use this skill to lift herself out of the depression.

Deeply depressed persons usually have difficulty in the verbal expression of their feelings because they are not in touch with those issues. These emotions are usually strongly negative ones such as anger, grief, and resentment. They are buried in the unconscious, repressed and frozen. The student sat before me with a stony expression on her face, her eyes downcast. It was a struggle for her to utter a sound. I suggested that it might be helpful to try to sculpt her feelings in clay. She nodded, and we arranged to see each other again. She returned the following week with a bust of Judas Iscariot, the apostle who betrayed Jesus. I was deeply impressed with her creation.

I took the sculpture home to show it to my wife, also a psychotherapist. I was interested to see her response to the work. She immediately threw a cloth over it and told me to remove it from our home. She was quite overcome by the powerful feelings of enmity rising from the sculpture. I encouraged the student to continue to bring me sculptures. It was revealing to note the subjects she chose and the moods that were revealed in her creations. Following the bust of Judas Iscariot she produced a sculpture I have since entitled "The Three Faces of Peter." In that one sculpture she developed three faces each characterized by the increasing agony Peter felt as he denied his relationship to Jesus.

The last of the young women's series of sculptures was one of love and intimacy. It was a work that included Jesus surrounded by his family. In the weeks that followed, her depression began to lift, and she began to develop the ability to verbalize her feelings.

A few days after my conversation with Fritz Jakobsson I visited the large community art gallery in Vasa as is my custom
each summer. I have always enjoyed looking at what the curator was showing from the permanent collection as well as seeing what was being featured this season. The gallery was now
exhibiting about one hundred paintings of the Finnish
painter Aulis Louko. I had not heard of Louko and decided
not to make any inquiries about his life until I examined his
art from Jakobsson's perspective. Over the next two hours I
looked at the paintings, always thinking in terms of: "What
does this tell me about the personality, the life style, and general attitude towards life, of this artist, Aulis Louko?"

The colours Louko used were predominantly heavy and
dark. There were many figures in his paintings, mainly adults.
I recall a painting of a young girl, her face etched by sadness.
That was as much as I could see, for none of the facial features
in Louko's subjects are pronounced. The girl is sprawled on a
couch, clutching a small teddy bear, looking desperately
unhappy. On the wall behind her is a picture of a bridal couple, presumably her parents. The title of the painting is "Alone
at Home."

As I looked at the various figures in Louko's paintings, I
initially characterized them as wooden. After a second examination I concluded they were individuals who were keeping a
tight rein on their feelings. One painting that impressed me
deeply was of a wedding party. The bride, groom, and others
are standing in a tight knot, a clutch of humans much too
close to each other. It is a painting of an enmeshed family
allowing no room for individual expression or opportunity
for personal growth.

After nearly two hours with Louko's paintings I came away
feeling morose and drained. I also had some quite definite

feelings about Aulis Louko. Almost without exception I felt the people in his paintings were depressed, their feelings repressed, their lives marked by quiet desperation. Based on my conversation with Jakobsson, I had to conclude that the artist was a depressed person. I noted that most of his work shown in the gallery had been completed in the 1970s. There was no evidence of work done after that time. I came to the conclusion that Aulis Louko had likely died by his own hand at the end of the decade.

On my way out I stopped at the front desk to chat with the young man, a personal friend, who was looking after the gallery that day. I asked Andre if he knew anything about the life of Louko. He knew a little. He told me that during the 1970s when Louko was producing most of his work, his paintings were not well received. Since then he has been recognized as an important artist. I inquired if he was still painting, as I wished to see some of his current work. Andre said: "Sorry to say, he committed suicide in 1977. He was just forty-one years old."

I left the gallery deeply moved. Later I discussed my experience with Fritz Jakobsson. I said that I had been told that Louko's art had not been well received by the community. "Not so," responded Fritz. "He was recognized as a talented artist, particularly by his colleagues. I recall talking to him myself, telling how impressed we all were with his work. But he could not accept our approval."

In a public lecture Louko once said: "The most important thing of all is that a piece of art expresses the truth. This truthfulness must not only be seen by the observer, but also be felt by him." His thoughts about the purpose of art were closely related to those of Fritz Jakobsson.

It is likely that if a thousand different artists were invited to share their definitions of the meaning of that elusive term, art, a wide variety of responses would be offered. Such questions are similar to issues about the meaning of life: What is death? What is the meaning and purpose of life? What is the meaning of meaning? Why were we created? Such questions defy complete answers, the questions being more important than the answers. If one has reached the maturity where such questions are raised, one begins to realize that ready-to-wear answers are unsatisfactory. Existential questions are related to existential anxiety, a form of anxiety which is incurable. Yet, we should not be prevented from experiencing the disturbing emotions of existential anxiety, a life experience that keeps us exploring, moving forward, growing, and developing.

Robert Fulghum, who has entertained and taught many through his writing, said that at public lectures when the speaker invited questions from the audience, he would always leap to his feet and ask: "What is the meaning of life?" Fulghum felt certain that he would always be entertained more than instructed by the answer he received. However, on one occasion he was so moved by a response that he included it, despite its length, in one of his books. No doubt the answer touched him deeply at that point in his life, connecting to life issues he was then facing. Similarly, the answer that Fritz Jakobsson gave me about the meaning of art touched me deeply, not only because it supported my view but also because it was a gift of insight, opening the way to further comprehension of the life of Benjamin Chee Chee, and in particular, Chee Chee the artist.

Understandably, Chee Chee was confused about his identity. Early in life we begin to develop a sense of identity, a product of the "who am I" search through contacts with parents, relatives, culture, and environment. In fact, Chee Chee grew up without parents, and his connection with his relatives and his culture was either tenuous or broken. His early life experiences were of loss and detachment. He was to make this scenario an ongoing experience in his life. He seemed unable to sustain long-term relationships. Although his introductory salutation, "My name is Benjamin, and I have a problem," seemed to be offered in jest, his problem of lost identity was deep, abiding, and painful. His problem, at the existential level, related to his identity as a human being. His inability to come to grips with this basic life task would finally destroy him.

Janet Clark, curator of the Thunder Bay Art Gallery, describes Chee Chee as being caught up in the "act of painting."[2] It is a telling phrase, suggesting that art took hold of Chee Chee and offered him a way leading to wholeness and away from lostness and confusion. Art held out to him the promise of an identity. He told an interviewer, "I wanted to be my own man. I wanted to develop a style that was so much my own that anyone looking at a painting by me would say at once, even if the work was unsigned, 'Now that was done by Benjamin Chee Chee.'"[3]

That wish was to become realized. He did become known by the uniqueness of his art forms. He insisted upon being recognized as an individual and despised any association with a group or a movement. He denied that he was led by artistic influences: "I don't like looking at other people's art."[4] He moved away from so-called "Indian Art" and legend painting. "Don't call me an Indian artist," he said. "I'm not. I think of myself as an Ojibway artist – a member of the Ojibway nation."[5] Yet in his compelling need to establish himself as an individual, he moved away from his Ojibway connection. His art became divorced from what is known as Ojibway art.

He was a member of the second generation of Woodland Indian painters, a movement that began in the early 1960s and at the time was one of the most sought after schools in Canada. Chee Chee, however, considered himself unique. Though he remained a member of the group, he moved into his own personal space and developed his individual style and focus. A *Globe* article described this difference: "While most of the other young Woodland Indian artists were content to follow the style of the movement's founder, Norval Morrisseau, in depicting myths and legends by direct and 'primitive' narrative means, Chee Chee pursued a more economical graphic style, a reduction of line and image more in keeping with the mainstream of international modern art. It was this search for stylistic breakthrough that made Chee Chee unique among his contemporaries."[6]

In a 1984 catalogue, curator Elizabeth McLuhan introduced Chee Chee as someone who, "above all, stripped Indian Art of its 'legend painting' trappings and returned to it the rigours of strong design and structural minimalism. 'Less was more' and his paintings evince a tireless interest in abstracting the essence of the image."[7] McLuhan describes the Black Geese Portfolio, completed shortly before his death: In a "continuing exploration of positive/negative space, his ability to concentrate in simple lyrical lines and monochromatic forms the vitality, grace, and humour of wildlife. His geese are always in motion, breathing, turning, flapping, flying or just taking off."[8]

Chee Chee, McLuhan noted "invested an enormous emotional significance in these images. The families of geese were a metaphor, a visual longing, for a family he never had." She refers to a series of paintings that include "Father and Son," "In Flight," "Mother and Son," "Family in Flight," and "Together."[9]

According to Ernie Bies, Chee Chee's close friend, "they represented himself and his Mom and Pop. One in particular showed the three of them flying high in the sky."[10] Chee Chee was not a reflective, discerning individual, nor was he a thinker. He appeared to be motivated by instincts and impulses. He seemed unaware of his inner dynamics and the meaning of his work. He steeled himself against pain, both physical and psychological. Frederick Brown described occasions in which he observed him stubbing burning cigarettes against his wrist, indicating that he felt no pain.

Though his persona often exuded warmth and congeniality, he seldom genuinely opened himself unless under the influence of alcohol. He was guarded to the point that he was unaware of the relationship of his art to his personal existence. He once denied that his art has anything to do with his past or with a search for his roots and his need for meaningful experiences; as far he was concerned, the rationale of his work remained superficial: "My drawing of birds and animals have no symbolic meaning from the past. To me they are creatures of the present and I draw them because I like their clean lines and beautiful shapes."[11] As T.S. Eliot has a characters say in "Dry Salvages," "We had the experience, but we missed the meaning."

There were moments when realization did break through. In a review in the *Ottawa Citizen* of Chee Chee's art, Nancy Baele writes, "The void he felt in not knowing his parents is integrated as a disjunctive element in many of his paintings, counterpointing a feeling of group harmony with an acute sense of isolation of an individual."[12] Baele goes on to give an example of the point she is making: "An acrylic on canvas in tones of gold and ochre has groupings of bison facing left with one lone animal facing in the opposite direction."[13] On one occasion, in the company of Frederick Brown, Chee Chee pointed to the lone bison and said, "That one is me!" However, there is no evidence that while he was creating the work he understood why he was doing what he was doing. Chee Chee had a preference for his abstract creations, although it was his birds that caught the buyers' eye. Norm Socha, owner of the Enook Gallery in Waterloo, Ontario, told me that if you covered a wall with his birds and another wall with his abstracts, the public's attention always focused on the bird paintings. Chee Chee was profoundly disappointed that his abstract creations were not as well received. Janet Clark comments: "Striving for an individual style, his early abstracts are, interestingly, reminiscent of work by a number of the Quebec painters and in particular Jacques Hurtubise, who came to prominence in the '60s and whose work was viewed in the public lexicon as modern. Chee Chee was certainly aware of what it was to be a 'modern' artist, and referred to himself as such."[14] Clark observed that a striking example of Chee Chee's abstract style, "Migration of 1973," included in the artist's initial exhibition, was purchased for inclusion in Canadian Indian Art '74, held at the Royal Ontario Museum in conjunction with the World Crafts Conference exhibition in Toronto that year. It was a source of considerable pride for Chee Chee.[15]

Generally he did not apply titles to his abstract work. "Migration" was an exception. Clark comments: "It suggests the migration pattern of geese or caribou or his own peripatetic wandering from town to town, and city to city, from Geraldton in Northern Ontario, to the Bear Island Reserve on Lake Temagami, to Montreal, and finally Ottawa, where he determined to devote himself full time to his artwork."[16] While it is unlikely that Chee Chee ever related "Migration" to his own restless search for identity and meaning, Clark, however, sensed the struggle that he was engaged in as he worked with his abstract material: "During this period he was attempting to express himself at a level and for reasons that were not as yet clear to him, yet he was willing to continue to engage in the struggle."[17]

Clark refers to a comment about the abstracts made by Tom Hill in a CBC audio production entitled *The Life and Death of Benjamin Chee Chee*: "They were indeed statements, they were intellectual paintings, that he really wanted to do. He felt that there was room for it. But of course he had to keep the wolves away, he had to put bread and butter on the table."[18] The demand for the more popular "Benny bird" creations caused his agents to nudge Chee Chee in a particular direction. This influence is noted in an angry article in the *Vancouver Sun* on 1 April 1977 by Wayne Edmonstone which suggests that Chee Chee was manipulated into producing art that would sell. Edmonstone condemns the art dealers and the government agency that represented Chee Chee. As a consequence of their demands, Edmonstone felt Chee Chee became dried up and burned out. His work became "simply an echo of the initial authentic sound of his message."[19] Edmonstone insinuates that what happened to Chee Chee in terms of viewing himself as an artist contributed to yet another layer of despair, which finally broke him: "a talented man who was still forced to struggle to find his own distinctive voice as an artist of stature, but of one who was in at least the first stages of giving up the struggle."[20] It was during this period that Chee Chee produced, at the urgent request of his dealer, five "Benny Birds" in one morning in the home of Frederick Brown. One wonders what effect that would have on a serious artist's psyche!

Moose, 1974

In 1983 the Thunder Bay Art Gallery acquired fifty-four of Chee Chee's paintings and prints. This work had been produced between 1973 and 1977 and, thanks to the effort of Norm Socha, maintained as a group. Included in this collection were eighteen acrylic paintings of geese images, the group now called the "Black Geese Portfolio."

Robert Houle, an artist and curator, first viewed the "Black Geese Portfolio" in 1978 and was deeply impressed with the work. Seeing the paintings again in 1990, he considered the possibility of developing an exhibition around them and did so at the Thunder Bay Art Gallery. From 16 October to 15 December 1991, works of Chee Chee from the gallery's permanent collection and other collections were exhibited. Houle recognized Chee Chee as a mature artist of note and saw the "Black Geese Portfolio" as produced "by a creative

Untitled, 1975

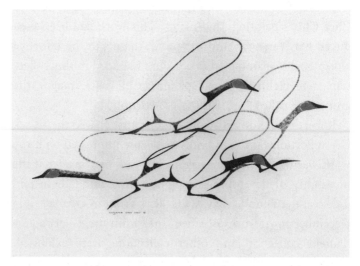

Dancing Geese, 1975

Untitled, 1975

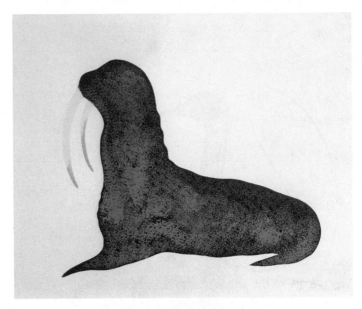

Untitled, 1975

persona at the pinnacle of his powers."[21] Edmonstone wrote his article shortly after Chee Chee's death, and it is likely that he had not had the opportunity to view the "Black Geese Portfolio."

It is necessary to examine Chee Chee's background in order to make an informed response to Edmonstone's probing question: "What can one possibly say – what can one possibly think – about the death of Ojibway artist Benjamin Chee Chee, who – at the age of 32 and at the height of a new-found success as an artist and printmaker – hanged himself in an Ottawa jail cell?" Thus we turn to Chee Chee's birthright in an attempt to comprehend those destructive dynamics.

4

OJIBWAY INHERITANCE

Don't call me an Indian artist! I'm not! I think of myself as
an Ojibway artist – a member of the Ojibway Nation.

–Benjamin Chee Chee

The history of the Ojibway people in North America reaches
back through centuries and, from the Ojibway perspective, to
the beginning of time. The Aboriginal people fully believed,
because of some terrible wrong their forbearers had committed against the Great Spirit, that the first earth had been
destroyed by a great flood. After a time a new earth had been
created in which they were given the right and the means to
exist. To support and guide this existence, a code had been
given to the Ojibway people to guide them on the path of
spiritual and ethical living. The living out of this religious
code was overseen by a spiritual being named Me-da-we-win.
This ever-present being acted as an intercessor between the
Great Spirit and the Ojibway. It was the Ojibway's task to
teach their offspring their code of life. It was passed from generation to generation through the oral tradition in the form
of stories and legends.

The History of the Ojibway People (first published in 1885
by the Minnesota Historical Society and reprinted in 1984)
was written by William W. Warren, who was born and spent

most of his life among the Ojibway of Lake Superior and the Upper Mississippi. His picture on the opening page of the book reveals a handsome young man with strong Native features from a mixed Ojibway and Euro-American heritage.

A Christian religious orientation is reflected in his description of the powerful connection the Great Spirit fostered with the Ojibway. Warren sees the nature of the relationship was that of a loving parent and a child: "Ke-che-mun-e-do (The Great Spirit) is the name used by Ojibways for the being equivalent to our God. They have another term which can hardly be surpassed by any one in the English language, for force, condensity, and expression, namely: Ke-zha-mune-do, which means pitying, charitable, overruling, guardian, and merciful Spirit; in fact, it expresses all the great attributes of the God of Israel. It is derived from Ke-zha-wand-e-se-roin, meaning, charity and kindness. Ke-zha-wus-so expressed the guardian feeling and solicitude of a parent toward its offspring, watching it with jealous vigilance from harm; and Shah-wau-je-gay, to take pity, merciful, with Mun-e-do (spirit)."[1]

Warren describes the feeling of reverence of the Ojibway for the Great Spirit: "There is nothing to equal the veneration with which the Native regards this unseen being. They seldom even mention his name unless in their Me-da-we and other religious rites, and in their sacrificial feasts; and then an address to him, however trivial, is always accompanied with a sacrifice of tobacco or some other article deemed precious by the Native. They never use his name in vain, and there is no word in their language expressive of a profane oath, or equivalent to the many words used in profane swearing by their more enlightened white brethren."[2]

The Ojibway nation forms one of the principal branches of the Algic people, a term derived from the word Algonquin, used by the early French discoverers to describe a tribe of aboriginals living on the St Lawrence River near Quebec. About 75,000 members of the Ojibway nation now live in Canada, and an equal number live in the United States. The Canadian Ojibway are located in about three dozen small reserves scattered throughout northern and southern Ontario.

The Ojibway are a proud people with a prestigious history. Since the seventeenth century they have been a part of the forces that moulded this country into a nation. Their story includes saving Canada, in company with their perennial enemy, the Iroquois, from the American army that invaded Canada in 1812. Had it not been for the Iroquois and the Ojibway, Canada might have been part of the United States long ago. Military historian G.F.G. Stanley credits the Iroquois with saving the nation. He writes: "If Canadians are disposed to think about the war of 1812 ... they cannot fail to recognize that it was during the critical years of this war, 1812, 1813, when the British troops were few in number and Britain was still heavily engaged upon the continent of Europe, that Iroquois Indians, both from Grand River and Caughnawaga, helped preserve their country's independence." Historian Peter Schmalz adds: "The same could be said for the Ojibway who had considerably less reason than the Iroquois to defend British subjects in Canada."[3] Men of the Ojibway nation were also involved in both world wars in the struggle to preserve Canada's way of life.

The *Handbook of Indians of Canada* lists over one hundred different names for Ojibway, though the derivation of the name has not been fully established. Various ethnic groups that came into contact with the Ojibway gave them different names: for example, the French called them Achipouie; the English, Chepawa; the Germans, Schipuwe; the Mohawk, Dewaganna; the Hyuron, Eskiaevonnon; the Caughawago,

Dwakane; the Sioux, Hahatonwa; the Fox, Kutaki; The
Winnebago, Iqegatce; the Tuscarora, Nwaka; the
Oneida, Twakanha; the Assiniboine, Wahkahtowah; and
the Ottawa, Ojibbewaig.[4] In the introduction to the 1984
edition of Warren's *History of the Ojibway People*, Roger
Buffalohead notes "Warren preferred to write the tribal
name as 'Ojibway' arguing that this spelling more closely
reflected in English how native speakers pronounced the
tribal name of their language. At the present time several
tribal names are used, including, but not limited to,
Chippewa, Ojibwa, and Anishinabe."[5]

The Ojibway were a powerful, aggressive nation of hunter-
warriors. For centuries they controlled a huge area of land in
North America, running the militant Iroquois out of what is
now known as Ontario and taking over their territory. By the
late eighteenth century the Ojibway held an expanse of land
from the eastern end of Lake Ontario westward to the vicini-
ty of Lake Winnipeg in Manitoba and the Turtle Mountains of
North Dakota. No other tribe in North America controlled
over such a huge area of the continent.

Peter S. Schmalz, in *The Ojibwa of Southern Ontario*, notes
that the holding of land is still dear to the heart of the
Ojibway:

The most potent symbol of southern Ojibwa identity is
the collective ownership of land. Ironically, the government's assimilationist policy of separating the Ojibwa
from these lands has contributed most to the retention
of their cultural identity. Historically, land has been the
primary issue in the Ojibwa's official dealings with other
native groups and especially with Europeans. The many
broken treaties connected to these lands have become
another important symbol of unity among the band

councils. The threat in the 1969 white paper to terminate collective ownership of reserves further stimulated interest in the land. For most Ojibwa land represents the major resource with which their leaders hope to overcome the economic disparity between Indians and whites. It is the locus of Indian social and cultural resources and the home base to which off reserve Ojibwa can withdraw from the white man's world. It is also the major link between the present and the past, providing the Ojibwa with a sense of historical experience.[6]

As warriors, the Ojibway were greatly feared by their enemies. From the first meeting, it is clear that the French explorer Samuel de Champlain was significantly impressed:

We met with three hundred men of a tribe named by us the Cheveux releves or "High Hairs," [Ojibwa] because they had them elevated and arranged very high and better combed than courtiers, and there is no comparison, in spite of the irons and methods these have at their disposal. This seems to give them a fine appearance. They wear no breech cloths, and are much carved about the body in divisions of various patterns. They paint their faces with different colours and have their nostrils pierced and their ears fringed with beads. When they leave their homes they carry a club. I visited them and gained some slight acquaintance and made friends with them. I gave a hatchet to their chief who was as happy and pleased with it as if I had made him some rich gift and, entering into conversation with him, I asked him about his country, which he drew for me with charcoal on a piece of tree-bark. He gave me to understand that they come to this place to dry the fruit called blueberries, to serve them as manna in the

winter when they can no longer find anything. For arms
they have only the bow and arrow."

In his search for the meaning of the word Ojibway, William
Warren discovered several possibilities. He noted that when
he questioned the elders on the subject, they avoided sharing
information and even tended to be misleading: "The answer
of their old men when questioned respecting the derivation
of their tribal name, is generally evasive." Warren believed
that they were attempting to mislead him when they tried to
convince him the word "ojib", which means literally "puckered up" or "drawn up," described the puckered seam on the
Ojibway moccasin.

Numerous stories are told of the Ojibway's indomitable
courage. Warriors would fight furiously against all odds. On
one occasion five Ojibway warriors were captured by French
troops. One of the warriors was killed, another avoided capture by cutting his own throat, and the other three were captured and put in irons. But the battle was not over. While
being transported by canoe, though weaponless and mana-
cled, the three captives freed themselves, killed the eight
French soldiers, and escaped.

A stubborn and adamant people, the Ojibway repudiated
any authority that tried to control them. This attitude was
portrayed in the confrontative words of an Ojibway chief following the defeat of the French by the British in the Seven
Years War. Chief Minavana spelled out the terms of their relationship to an English fur trader: "Englishman, although you
have conquered the French, you have not yet conquered us!
We are not your slaves. These lakes, these woods and mountains were left to us by our ancestors. They are our inheritance, and we will part with them to none. Your nation sup-

poses that we, like the white people, cannot live without bread
– and pork – and beef! But you ought to know, that He, The
Great Spirit and Master of Life, has provided food for us, in
these spacious lakes, and on these woody mountains."[8]

Not only aggressive fighters, the Ojibway were also artful,
ingenious warriors with an inborn ability to overcome the
insurmountable. Ojibway Chief Minweweh bore a passionate
hatred for the English. It was his intention to capture one of
their strongest forts in the Upper Great Lakes. Its strong walls
would be difficult to assail, perhaps even impossible without
great loss of life. Chief Minweweh, a wily, experienced warrior, nevertheless felt compelled to take the fort. He carefully
planned a surprise attack using the ploy of a lacrosse game.

Historian Alexander Henry was present and watched this
horrendous happening. Eventually saved by an Ojibway he
had befriended, Henry described the attack:

> In the ardour of the contest, the ball … if it cannot be
> thrown to the goal desired, is struck in any direction by
> the adversary. At such a moment, therefore, nothing could
> be less liable to excite premature alarm, than that the ball
> should be tossed over the pickets of the fort, nor that hav-
> ing fallen there, it should be followed on the instant, by all
> engaged in the game, as well the one party as the other, all
> eager, all struggling, all shouting, all in the unrestrained
> pursuit of a rude athletic exercise. Nothing could be less
> fitted to excite premature alarm – nothing, therefore,
> could be more happily devised, under the circumstances,
> than a stratagem like this; and this was, in fact, the strata-
> gem which the Indians had employed, by which they had
> obtained possession of the fort, and by which they had
> been enabled to slaughter and subdue its garrison.[9]

To support the warriors in this attack Ojibway women stood near the fort gates with weapons hidden under their blankets. Between ninety and a hundred soldiers made up the garrison. In the fight that followed, seventy were killed and the rest taken prisoner and held for ransom.

Yet to view this hunter-warrior culture as an aggressive, blood-thirsty society, intent only upon making war, would be to completely misunderstand these people. They were a hunter-warrior culture, but they were also a cultured people deeply rooted in a pantheistic view of nature that affected every segment of their lives. Entrenched in the world of the numinous, the Ojibway were guided and controlled by a belief system that required that because they were creations of the Great Spirit, they must respect themselves as persons of worth. Valuing themselves as creations of the spirit, they were able to see others in the same light. Their theological beliefs, and the ways in which those beliefs impacted and influenced their behaviour are closely related to the basic tenets of the great religions of the West but in particular to the religions of the East: Hinduism, Buddhism, Confucianism, Taoism, and Shintoism.

The Ojibway believed that spiritual beings lived among them in various forms and that these spiritual entities were to be revered. The Ojibway treasured the presence of these spirits and looked to them as the source of internal nourishment, strength, and wisdom. In *Ojibwa Myths and Legends*, the authors Coleman, Froger, and Eich introduce a leading spiritual being named Nanabozho:

The old Ojibwa liked to tell us about Nanabozho, the one-time principal figure in Algonquian mythology, legendary history, and the Grand Medicine Society. But when confronted with the question "Who is Nanabozho?", they looked perplexed. They accept Nanabozho and his characteristics, inconsistent as these may be, and thus they found it difficult to reply. Most of them said he is a powerful manido or spirit being. Some said he is the "Great Rabbit." One woman said, "He is both human and super-human." One of our youngest informants spoke of him as a "superman", and still another said, "Nanabozho is an ordinary Indian and an Indian extraordinary". Almost unanimously Nanabozho was mentioned as a brother to the animals, the plants, the trees, and the many different aspects of nature. As the legends show, Nanabozho has all of these characteristics and still others.[10]

Nanabozho was the source of many gifts. He is remembered as the spirit who gave them the gift of corn. He was told by his grandmother that she had a dream in which she learned of a young brave named Mandomin who lived across the Great Sea. In the dream the grandmother was told that Nanabozho must conquer Mandomin for the sake of the Ojibway. Nanabozho crossed the water and mountains until he met a tall brave in green robes. This was Mandomin. The two wrestles, and Nanabozho finally won. "When Mandomin saw that he had lost, he spoke to Manabozho. 'Since you are better and stronger than I am, I surrender to you. I will no longer be a brave, but I shall be changed into a stalk of green corn. I will give myself up to you so that you can return to your people.' Mandomin then taught Nanabozho how he [Mandomin] was to be buried. He first taught him how to prepare the soil. When the corn came up, it was very beneficial as food. That is how the Ojibway got corn to eat."[11]

Through stories of Nanabozho, the Ojibway were taught the code of behaviour that was acceptable and that which was intolerable. In another legend Nanabozho is presented in disgrace because he broke the Ojibway cultural taboo against incest: In this legend, Nanabozho, a widower with two daughters and a son, fakes his own death, then returns in disguise and marries his older daughter.

> One day Nanabozho and his boy went out hunting beaver. Nanabozho boasted and called the boy "son and brother-in-law." When they returned from the hunt, the boy asked his sister, "Why does he call me son and brother-in-law?" The sisters wondered. They decided to look for a scar which their father had on his head. They knew that their father had such a scar. When Nanabozho was sleeping, the girls found it. Then they ran away and left Nanabozho. Nanabozho did not know what to do, so he started travelling. He went from village to village. He asked little children, "Have you heard anything about Nanabozho?" "Yes," they answered, "we heard that Nanabozho married his own daughter." Everybody seemed to know of his shame and so he kept on going. No one knows what became of him.[12]

The authors of *Ojibway Myths and Legends* comment: "The Ojibwa beliefs about Nanabozho need to be viewed in relation to the traditional belief in a large number of manidos or spirit beings (good and evil) that were thought to exist everywhere in nature – in the animals, birds, trees, and odd-shaped rock, the waterfalls, thunder and lightning, the winds and the cardinal directions. The heavens and the earth and the layers above and below the earth were all the abode of manidos.

This entire concept rested on the belief that the natural and the supernatural were inseparable. Thus it can be seen how the natural world would be considered a source of spirit power."[13] Though the Ojibway lived in the natural world, they were rooted in the world of the spirit, a deeply spiritual people. Not only did they believe that the Great Spirit was to be found in the sun, the moon, the stars, in all things throughout the universe, the earth and all human and non-human creatures but – of greater personal significance – the Great Spirit was to be found within themselves.

In the development of his doctoral dissertation "Native Values in a Non-Native World," David Hodson has drawn on a number of studies establishing that Native spirituality was far advanced. According to Hodson, the teaching of the great faiths that the Creator is to be found within one's own psyche has for centuries been a basic tenet of aboriginal belief as well. Believers experienced the truth that the Great Spirit lived within their own being. Also deeply rooted in the belief system of aboriginal people was the need to be aware that one dwells within the Great Spirit. To face the existential issues of life – that is, purpose, meaning, and direction – one must try to comprehend the Great Spirit. In one's thoughts, feelings, behaviour, and belief, one must live the Great Spirit, that is, live as if one were the Great Spirit. It was accepted that the Great Spirit created men, women, children, animals, trees, and the whole of nature with the intent of remaining an active part of creation forever. Everything was alive with the spirit of creation.[14]

The Great Spirit was the model of life and how to live it. There were times when they would fail in their intent, but they were always mindful that the fault lay within them and not in the absence of the Great Spirit. They were responsible for their own downfall but were encouraged by the spirit to overcome these failings, which were to be seen as challenges. The elders, those who had achieved spiritual wisdom, taught that the purpose of the obstacles encountered along the path of life was to develop strength and steadfastness. These hardships developed because of a lack of spirituality that caused an imbalance in people's lives, causing them to become weak and to fall down. Though they were responsible for the creation of these imbalances which led to self-destructive behaviours, the Great Spirit continued to be involved, caring, supportive, and always empathic, guiding them back to the path of balance again.

Hodson differentiates between Native prayer and Christian prayer: "Native prayer is an effort to directly access one's own spiritual essence, to be at one with oneself and thereby with the world. Christian prayer is typically directed to an external cosmic entity. Thus, for the Native, the 'spiritual' world and its powers dissolves the Christian distinction between the internal and the external, between the subject and the object."[15] The function of prayer was to develop and nurture the relationship that existed between the individual and the Great Spirit. As this relationship flourished, one was enabled to become more fully in touch with inner spiritual resources.

The belief that not only does one live within the spirit but that indeed the whole of life rests within the spirit fostered a more ethical life and enriched personal relationships. Hodson comments that Native people viewed everything in life as having vital worth. Everything and every person had a unique function to perform. Though uniqueness was recognized, it was also understood that no function was more important than any other. Equality reigned throughout creation.

Native belief was that a sense of health and well-being was

to be celebrated and enjoyed but only if that quality of life was shared with others. It was also necessary that the environment be cared for and respected. If the environment was hurt and destroyed, the same fate would befall humankind. From the beginning of time aboriginal people referred to the earth as Mother Earth, who had given birth to all things. The sun was believed to be the Father, because he was needed for nurturing and development. Humankind must love and revere their creators and be responsible for the care and well-being of Mother Earth and all she produced. Failure to meet one's obligations to Mother Earth created personal suffering.

Traditionally, Natives believed that Mother Earth could not be owned or possessed. The land was held in trust and belonged to no one. Mother Earth might be used for purposes related to humankind's nurturance, overall well-being, and existence. If used for creative purposes, Mother Earth would provide the nourishment that enabled humankind to be strong and to flourish. If the environment was used for destructive purposes, humankind in turn would be destroyed.

The presence of pollution in the environment is evidence today that Mother Earth has not been used with care and respect. When the earth becomes sick, humans become diseased. Throw a stone in a pond, and the pond and everything it contains, and the land that embraces it, will be affected. When a butterfly flaps its wings, it will affect the air currents throughout the world, even though in a minuscule way. Traditionally, Natives believed in the ripple effect. They believed that when any part of nature was troubled, humans would be affected. The cause of illness and personal tragedy was rooted in being out of harmony with themselves, with nature, and with the Great Spirit. The well-being of the human spirit was intricately interwoven with the rest of nature.

Killing was acceptable if the act was carried out for good
reason. The killing of animals for food was an acceptable act.
Before and after the act was committed, the hunter was
required to give thanks for the gift of the animal. Through its
death, it had provided nourishment. As Hodson notes: "Such
prayer expresses respect for the animal and the plant members of the earth's 'family'; it is believed that they voluntarily
give their lives for the continued well-being of humans. Thus
Natives believe that humans must live in harmony with their
fellow creatures in order to enjoy a life of peace and prosper-
ity."[16] Native philosophy insisted that natural creatures and
objects should be destroyed only for one reason – that is, for
a basic requirement of life, the food to survive.[17] Killing for
the sake of killing was a violation of the laws of nature.

There existed no division between humankind, animals,
and the environment. All were one, creations of the Great
Spirit: "both living and dead human beings may assume the
form of animals. So far as appearance is concerned, there is no
hard and fast line that can be drawn between an animal form
and a human form, because of the possibility of metamor-
phosis. In perceptual experience, what looks like a bear may
be an animal, but under some conditions, it is a human being.
The outward appearance of persons is not stable. What per-
sists, and gives continuity to being, is the vital part, spirit."[18]

This basic value of equality arising out of the belief that all
of life is an expression of the creative spirit focuses on the
need for community within oneself, with others, and with the
environment. Often in a non-native culture the emphasis is
on individual achievement for the purpose of gaining power
and control. In the lives of the aboriginal people, the individual was not central. It was the quality of community life that
was the predominant concern. Foremost in community life

was taking care of others. Life was to be lived for the welfare of others. The self was insignificant. Cooperation with others at every level of life was encouraged and taught to the children through the parents' example. Class differences did not exist in aboriginal society. Though one person might have more ability than the others, that did not make him or her better than the others. It was expected that the superior ability would be used for the good of the community. The value of integrity controlled the behaviour of one person to another, to the community, and to the environment in which one lived. Integrity was the manifestation of the Great Spirit that influenced human behaviour in community.

Hodson describes the generosity evident in personal relationships among traditional aboriginals. They shared whatever they had with each other. Property was held in common. The need to share was a response to their belief in the omnipresence of the Great Spirit: as the individual shared with others, he believed he was sharing with the Great Spirit: "The individual and society are viewed as one, to feed and provide for others as one would for oneself, is to act in harmony with the universe's intricate design. The individual grows as others grow, and contribute to 'the spirit of things', which is the spirit of life itself."[19] In 1709 Jesuit Father Antoine Silvy observed that one became a chief only "by the deeds he had done, by the friendships he struck when young, and by the gifts he gives ... Usually these chiefs are the worst clad of the tribe as they give everything to be liked."[20]

For the traditional Native, Hodson says, spirituality is a way of life: "It is self-discipline in body, word and mind, self-development and self-purification. The Great Spirit, the spirit of all Native existence, is all life. God flows through all, nature and the universe, such that each entity, living and non-living, is an integral part of the universe's intricate design. All life, all things, all spirits, the Great Spirit, are within humans. In the Native view, then, people must respect the responsibility and freedom they have in order to understand and 'know' themselves for the betterment of society."[21]

Though we may not accept the theological doctrine of pantheism, "God is in everything, everything is God," it is difficult to deny there is a connectedness between all things and all beings, human and animal. In our own cultural history there have been periods when we have strongly experienced that connectedness. In a course on personality and spirituality I introduced this idea of oneness and detachment experienced through various decades from the 1960s through to the '90s. For my purposes here I focus on the 1960s and '70s.

From the conservative 1950s we moved into the expansive '60s, impelled by a young people's movement seeking greater openness, freedom of expression, and togetherness. The winds of radical change affected education, values, and lifestyles. The Beatles emerged from Liverpool to introduce a new type of music. During that period I heard sociologist Virginia Satir identify the world as Spaceship Earth. We were existing together and we needed to accept our interdependence if we were to survive the journey. Satir was reflecting an idea expressed by others in different ways. Fritz Perls, a Freudian psychiatrist, introduced Gestalt psychotherapy while Eric Berne, a Canadian psychiatrist, popularized Transactional Analysis. Both types of psychotherapy enabled individuals to rid themselves of their defensive styles to become more open and trusting, developing feelings of responsibility towards others and the total environment. The concepts being introduced by these teachers were very close to what Hodson describes as the teaching of the Great Spirit.

The idealism of the '60s did not survive long. At the beginning of the '70s the narrow, restricted "Me" generation emerged. But now, in this present age, we are indeed realizing that we live together on Spaceship Earth. A number of experiences, for better or for worse, remind us of this. A woman somewhere deep in China is smitten by a coronavirus, and Canada's most populated city is threatened with something like the Plague. A terrorist bomb explodes in a place most of would have trouble finding on the map, and we flinch and think about changing our travel plans. At one time on the Grand Banks of Newfoundland there were so many fish it was difficult to propel a boat through the water. After many years of over-fishing, we are astonished that the fish are no longer there. We fail to nurture the earth and cannot understand why we have dust storms and the crops wither in the ground.

Nelson Mandela, incarcerated for over twenty-five years in South Africa, emerges from his prison cell to bring freedom to his nation, and inspires us to live nobler lives. A man who lost everything in the concentration camps of World War II writes a book about meaning that has sold nine million copies and is still in print; Viktor Frankl's work continues to influence us all in our search for meaning. Lessons of our connectedness taught by the elders in aboriginal society are still being taught today.

A young Native, formerly one of my students, now living on a reserve in Alberta, called the elders "living libraries." Did these teachers affect the shaping of Benjamin Chee Chee's life? What were his values? Was he introduced to the ancient legends by his mother, or by the elders? On Bear Island where he was raised, did he experience a closeness with the Great Spirit among the natural wonders of the spirit's creation?

Some of the personal characteristics revealed in Chee Chee's life and work reflect his roots in Ojibway culture. His art expresses his knowledge of nature and his love and reverence for it. His work was not simply painting or drawing birdlike forms; it emerged from deep within him. Someone must have led him into that experience enabling him to become so deeply immersed in those dynamic inner workings.

In character and lifestyle, Chee Chee was in many ways still part of a hunter-warrior culture. He was unconventional, refusing to be controlled by white society's idea of appropriate behaviour. He was a fighter, never compliant, a maverick with an unpredictable, unyielding personality. His stubbornness was an essential element in the mix that was Benjamin Chee Chee. That proud spirit carried him through difficult times but also plunged him into torment.

Chee Chee revered and loved Native ways. He acknowledged that his adult identity was connected to being born Ojibway. But he inherited not only a cherished place in the Ojibway nation: he was also born into a culture destined to introduce him to a life of misery and hopelessness. He was born a Canadian Native during the twentieth century.

The following chapter describes his legacy as a Native Canadian – such a destructive experience that it would lead to his death.

5

CANADIAN NATIVE
INHERITANCE

If I were to accept the bothersome term Indian problem, I would have to accept it in the light of the fact that our most basic problem is gaining respect, respect on an individual basis that would make possible acceptance for us as an ethnic group. Before this is possible, the dignity, the confidence and pride of the Indian people must be restored.

–Harold Cardinal, *The Unjust Society*

AN EDUCATION IN DESPAIR

It was of vital concern to Benjamin Chee Chee that he be recognized as a member of the Ojibway nation. At his best his life was focused on that cherished reality. The values he inherited from the Ojibway nation were treasures that continually enriched his life. These included his love and reverence for nature, his drive and determination to prevail against unassailable odds, and his compelling need to be creative.

However, another cultural context into which he was born would contaminate the values guiding his life as an Ojibway. Experiences from that second culture, fed into his life from birth, guaranteed a despairing and arduous life's journey. Chee Chee was a Native raised on a Canadian Indian reservation. This circumstance exposed him to elements that would play a significant role in the processes that eventually led to his destruction. He was born into a culture where he would struggle in vain to find acceptance, or a place where he felt safe. Though his inheritance as an Ojibway would enrich his life, his identity as a Canadian Native would rob him of those values and leave him exposed and empty.

Geoffrey York's aptly titled *The Dispossessed: Life and Death in Native Canada*, the story of the ongoing genocide of a people, graphically describes the incomprehensible losses suffered by members of the Aboriginal population as the consequence of trying to exist in the Canadian culture. There is ample evidence to support the claim that the Canadian culture is characterized by ignorance and gross insensitivity towards its Native population. The material in York's study staggers the imagination and leaves the reader angry and ashamed. It should be required reading for every Canadian.

To comprehend the life and death of Benjamin Chee Chee, it is imperative to open the dark side and view the qualities of life he inherited as a Canadian Native.[1] For generations sincere efforts have been made by government officials, politicians, Native leaders, and caregivers (professional and otherwise) to right the wrongdoing and bring about positive change. Some progress has been made, although forward movement is often difficult to detect because the psychic wounds inflicted on the Native population are deep, and for some beyond healing. More generations will pass before a complete and holistic healing can take place. It will become a reality only with fulfilment of many conditions. One stands out above all others: Canadian Natives must become respected as persons, not only by Canadians but by Natives themselves.

There are three categories of Native people in Canada: Status Indians, Métis or Non-Status Indians, and Inuit.

Status Indians hold membership in a band and consequently have certain rights under the Indian Act and individual treaties. There are 608 registered bands across Canada occupying or having access to 2,274 reserves of varying size. About 58.1 per cent of Status Indians actually live on reserves or Crown land. There are about 624,000 Status Indians in Canada.

Métis or Non-Status Indians are Native people who still identify themselves as Indians. The Métis originally lost their Indian status because they intermarried with other groups, namely, French and English. Non-Status Indians waived their rights of status for a number of reasons: to gain the right to vote (prior to 1960); to own land or business off the reservation; simply because of failure to register. There are about 152,800 Métis or Non-Status Indians in Canada.

Inuit (the name Eskimo is now rejected by these Natives) Native Canadians number about 57,000 men, women and children.

Christopher Columbus in a message to the king and queen of Spain described his response to North American Natives: "I swear to your Majesties that there is not a better people in the world than these, more affectionate, affable, or mild. They love their neighbour as themselves, and they always speak smilingly."[2] Since the invasion by the white race into their domain, Natives have had little to smile about. The population of the Canadian Natives was conservatively numbered to be about 500,000 when the Europeans arrived some five hundred years ago. Diseases introduced by the white race such as smallpox, tuberculosis, influenza, scarlet fever, and measles, combined with massacres, cut the population drastically. From the 1400s on the Native population was reduced to about 100,000. *The Report of the Royal Commission on Aboriginal Peoples* observes: "A census estimate of the size of the Aboriginal population in Canada in 1871 places the number at 102,000. It would take more than 100 years – until the early 1980s – before the size of the Aboriginal population again reached the 500,000 mark. Since that time the Native population has developed at twice the national average."[3]

John Beaver, an Ojibway born and raised on the Alderville Indian Reserve situated on the shores of Rice Lake, Ontario, is one of the few Canadian Natives who has been successful in the Canadian business world. John Beaver is persuaded that the Canadian Native is much worse off now than when Canada became a nation in 1867. Referring to the Canadian government in its relationship to the Canadian Native, he told me, "You have to say they [Canadian government] are abject failures when the average condition of the Native is worse now than it was at Confederation time. Certainly in terms of starvation they are no worse. But in terms of the breakdown we have been talking about [suicide, homicide, alcoholism], certainly in terms of their mental condition, and in many other ways, they are worse off." A study of the literature, including York's book, supports Beaver's statement.

Harold Cardinal, a well-known Native spokesman, writes in his book, *The Unjust Society*, "If I were to accept the bothersome term Indian problem, I would have to accept it in the light of the fact that our most basic problem is gaining respect, respect on an individual basis that would make possible acceptance for us as an ethnic group. Before this is possible, the dignity, the confidence and pride of the Indian people must be restored. No genuine Indian participation in the white world can be expected until the Indian is accepted by himself and by the non-Indian as an Indian person, with an Indian identity."[4] Though Cardinal wrote those words over thirty years ago, the issue of personal respect still lies at the root of the Canadian Natives' difficulties. Self-acceptance, respect, recognition by others, a personal sense of worth, value, meaning, or direction in life all seem to be missing from most Canadian Natives' experience. Because of these missing elements, their condition of life has become one of the most deplorable in the world.

From the beginning of its relationship with the Native population, the intention of the government of Canada was to assimilate Natives into the white population. Natives would become like us, "a brown white person." Natives were considered to be savage, uneducated, and pagan. The Canadian government would not only civilize and educate these primitive people but would also save their souls.

It is abundantly clear that post-Confederation government policy was to absorb the Aboriginal culture into the dominant white culture: "In the first few decades of the life of the new Canadian nation, when the government turned to address the constitutional responsibility for Indians and their lands assigned by the Constitution Act, 1867, it adopted a policy of assimilation ... the roots of this policy were in the pre- Confederation period. It was a policy designed to move communities, and eventually all Aboriginal peoples, from their helpless 'savage state to one of self-reliant civilization' and thus to make in Canada but one community – a non-Aboriginal, Christian one."[5]

To realize these goals, lands were set aside to be occupied only by Natives. Schmalz points out in *The Ojibwa of Southern Ontario*, "The reserves were established to convert the Indians from heathen to Christians and from hunters to farmers. Schools were built in an attempt to accelerate the cultural transition, and some children were sent to residential schools to isolate them from parental influence."[6]

The general view was (and to a considerable extent this view still prevails) that Natives are inferior to white persons. Consequently Natives needed to be transformed, their lives reshaped, their destinies redirected. The benevolent government would take over this responsibility. Control over their lives was taken out of Native hands.

The attitude of paternalism was shaped into a genuinely well-meaning program with the purpose of caring and protecting the needy Native. We now know paternalism is ruinous for the one forced to remain a child. This attitude on the part of the Government of Canada was ultimately destructive for the Canadian Native. Chief Wakegijig of the Wikwemikong Indian reserve on Manitoulin Island, Ontario, the site of a suicide epidemic among young Natives, has said that paternalism rid his people of any feeling for work, and consequently of any sense of worth, purpose, and meaning: "The government has destroyed the values of our people by giving them handouts all the time instead of economic opportunities." Ben Belanger, Ontario welfare administrator for Sudbury and Manitoulin, supported Chief Wakegijig's sentiment, adding that once the government started down that road, it would discover there was no end to it. Belanger said in 1976, "We've been paternal with the Indians and that is not the right way to build self-sufficiency."[7] His words continue to be prophetic. Paternalism is a trap in which both the trapper and the victim become snared.

Mary Percy Jackson, for fifty years a resident physician at Keg River, five hundred miles northwest of Edmonton, Alberta, observed in a convocation address in 1976 at the University of Alberta: "The white man's welfare system has reduced Canada's Native population to a state of dependency and inferiority." Long before the introduction of old age pensions and family allowances, she said, Natives were self-supporting and sharing as a community of neighbours. "But the white social worker soon worked a quick social revolution.

The first time a trapper came in from the bush with his furs to be greeted by his wife with the information that she had managed to talk the welfare man out of more money than he had made in a two week hunt, some of his pride and self-respect was lost."[8]

By the time of Confederation, a fully developed government policy had been established that gave the Government of Canada the power to legislate all things pertaining to the lives of Natives and the land set aside for them. The Department of Indian Affairs was created to manage their affairs, that is, to parent the undisciplined, uneducated, and uncivilized children. The government believed its policy would be beneficial. But despite the government's belief that it had the Natives' best interest at heart, the policy was paternalism at its worst, created out of ignorance and bigotry, and resulted in a quagmire. It would lead the Natives into deep suffering and devastation. Today Natives continue to struggle for self-determination, and the government continues to struggle to disentangle itself. Over a hundred years has passed with limited progress over the political issues. But what of the human devastation and hope for change at the fundamental human level? The heart and mind despairs.

Until very recent times, though numerous attempts have been made to create useful change, there was always one important omission: Canadian Natives were not included in the planning and development of their own lives. The reserve system had the same effect as a Siberian Gulag. It separated Natives from the ongoing economic, social, educational, and political development of the nation. They were treated as a subject people, their language, their customs, their knowledge, and their religion ignored and mocked.

As a consequence of misguided government policy, the

Canadian Native has emerged as a sorry figure to whom Canadian citizens respond with a mixture of negative and positive feelings. Harold Cardinal accurately describes this attitude: "Today, most Canadians are either indifferent to Indians or hate them or pity them. The worst of the three is the man who pities the Indian, for he denies the object of his pity the opportunity to be a man."[9]

A study on Native youth in Edmonton by the Alberta Department of Culture, Youth and Recreation in 1971 pointed to the difficulties that Native youth have in a society dominated by the white culture by referring to a psychological concept known as the "looking glass self."[10] This concept identifies the process of adopting behaviours and lifestyles in which individuals mirror their understanding of how others feel about them: "Discrimination against Natives has resulted because of employers' unfavourable experiences with Native employees. This process has developed an unfavourable stereotype of the Indian workers, who, in reacting to the employers' treatment and expectation, have in turn developed attitudes and behaviour that tend to reinforce this stereotype."[11] The stereotype that is reinforced is that the Native Canadian is irresponsible, unreliable, lazy, drunk, stupid, lacking in determination and will power, and bereft of values and integrity.

This same stereotype is related to the emergence of anti-social behaviour that has led to the incarceration of large numbers of the Native population. An examination of the Canadian penal record raises questions about why Canadian Natives are so unlawful, and why the numbers of Natives in jails and prisons are over-represented when compared to those of non-Natives. The National Indian Council estimated that one-third of the total provincial inmate population of

Canadian correction institutions is made up of Native people although Natives constitute only 4 per cent of the population. In some provinces the percentage of Native people in the prison population is unbelievably high. Natives and Métis make up 10 per cent of the population of Manitoba, yet 60 per cent of the prison population is Native. In Newfoundland and New Brunswick the percentage of Natives in jail is four to six times higher than the provincial average for non-Natives. In a provincial correctional centre in Saskatchewan 75 per cent of male inmates are Native. In the women's correctional centre, 85 per cent of inmates are Native.

George Manuel and Michael Posluns explain the extremely high level of incarceration among Natives: "native people are not greater criminals than whites. Most of the offenses for which Indians are jailed are either petty offenses or crimes of passion; it is rare for an Indian to be charged with armed robbery, kidnapping, or any offence that is a serious threat to the larger society. We are jailed for minor offenses that stem from the frustrations of living in a racist and colonial society. Sometimes these frustrations boil over and we take them out on the people who are closest to us."[12]

Geoffrey York reports that the number of Native prisoners in jails across Canada has doubled in the past three decades and he expects the tendency to continue. He presents one particularly troubling fact: "One statistic, above all others, captures the full meaning of the great lock-up of the Aboriginal people in this country. It has been calculated that an ordinary Indian boy in Saskatchewan who turned sixteen in 1976 has a seventy percent probability of being thrown into jail by the age of twenty-five." He cites the report of a committee of the Canada Bar Association in 1988 decrying this situation: "Prison has become, for young native men, the promise of a just society which high school and college represent for the rest of us. Placed in historical context, the prison has become for many young native people the contemporary equivalent of what the Indian residential school represented for their parents."[13]

The root of the residential school system is to be found in 1879 when Sir John A. Macdonald's government, influenced by the Roman Catholic and Methodist churches, appointed Nicholas Flood Davin to report on Industrial Schools in the United States and bring in recommendations for similar institutions to be tailored for the training of Canadian Natives. *The Report of the Royal Commission on Aboriginal Peoples* comments: "Davin called for the 'application of the principle of industrial boarding schools' – off-reserve schools that would teach the arts, crafts and industrial skills of a modern economy. Children, he advised, should be removed from their homes, as 'the influence of the wigwam was stronger than that of the (day) school', and 'be kept constantly within the circle of civilized conditions' – the residential school – where they would receive the 'care of a mother' and an education that would fit them for a life in a modernizing Canada."[14]

The residential school system was to become one of the most damaging examples of motherhood yet conceived. Prior to World War II, Native children were required to attend residential schools operated by religious denominations. York writes: "The government, like the churches, believed the Indian culture was 'barbaric' and 'savage.' The federal authorities were determined to transform the Indian children into faithful Christians who would abandon their traditional native spiritual beliefs."[15]

The residential school experience fragmented the family experience. For at least ten months of the year, children did not see their parents during life-stage periods when the father and mother are needed most. That separation would create psychological problems that would continue to contaminate the individual's personality throughout his or her life. As a former student of the residential school system, Harold Cardinal is harshly critical of the quality of teachers who were appointed to teach the Native children, referring to them as "misfits and second-raters." He declares: "The residential schools even failed in their first purposes ... turning out good little Christians. They alienated the child from his own family, and from his own way of life without in any way preparing him for a different society; they alienated the child from his own religion and turned his head resolutely against the confusing substitute the missionaries offered. Worst of all, the entire misconceived approach, the illogical (to the Indian children) disciplines offered, the failure to relate the new education in any pragmatic way to their lives turned the child against education, prevented him from seeing or appreciating the benefits of real education." Cardinal concludes: "For the Canadian Indian, the lack of educational opportunities prior to the mid-fifties marks those generations as a time of neglect which is still taking its toll."[16]

York describes the educational experience of the Ojibway children of Sabaskong Bay, Ontario: "For almost a century, outsiders had controlled the education of Sabaskong Bay. Missionaries set up residential schools where the Ojibway children were confined day and night, with no family contact, while they were indoctrinated with the religion and culture of the white man. They were separated from their parents and prohibited from speaking Ojibway."[17]

To destroy a culture, it is imperative to obliterate its language. In that respect part of the process of assimilation has been successful. York reports that of the fifty-three Native languages in Canada today fifty are in danger of becoming extinct. Thirteen of these languages are considered extremely endangered as they are spoken by fewer than one hundred persons.[18] Despite its primary intention, the residential school experience turned out to be an experience in brainwashing. The use of Native languages by the students in the residential school system was prohibited. Students were not allowed to speak even to their own blood relatives in a Native tongue while in residence. Anyone found speaking a Native language would be severely punished.

Mary Carpenter, an Inuit, told of her agonizing experiences as a young girl in Anglican and Roman Catholic residential schools: "After a lifetime of beating, going hungry, standing in a corridor on one leg, and walking in the snow with no shoes for speaking Inuvialuktun, and having a heavy, stinging paste rubbed on my face, which they did to stop us from expressing our Eskimo custom of raising our eyebrows for 'yes' and wrinkling our noses of 'no,' I soon lost the ability to speak my mother tongue. When a language dies, the world it was generated from is broken down too."[19]

A Mi'kmaq poet, Rita Joe, expresses the pathos she feels at the loss of her ability to express herself in her own language:

I lost my talk
The talk you took away.
When I was a little girl
At Shubenacadie school.
You snatched it away:
I speak like you
I think like you
I create like you

The scrambled ballad, about my world.
Two ways I talk
Both ways I say
Your way is more powerful
So gently I offer my hand and ask,
Let me find my talk
So I can teach you about me.[20]

Residential schools founded by Protestant and Catholic missionaries were powerful agents of change with regard to language, life style, belief systems, values, and cultural preferences. The educational system was used to transform the Native and demolish the infrastructure that formerly supported his or her life. The residential school system was a dominant institution in Native communities across Canada from the late nineteenth century until the 1960s.

We tend to think of education as an enriching resource that leads to a fuller mature life. In retrospect the residential school system was a sinister influence, spoiling the lives of many young Natives. But the story does not end there. The conditioning process that warped the lives of many continues to do so into the twenty-first century. Though the schools no longer exist, their contaminating influence continues to disrupt the lives of many of the Native adults forced as children to attend them. And not only the victims are affected but also those whose lives they touch.

For years there have been shocking revelations of widespread sexual abuse in the residential school system operated by religious denominations. An example of the extent of the abuse emerged following an RCMP investigation based on the research of a family therapist in the small logging town of Lytton, in the Fraser Canyon of British Columbia. Many of

the therapist's clients were Natives from the Nl'akapxm
Nation living on a reserve near Lytton. These Natives suffered
from problems of alcoholism, depression, and suicidal behaviour. In her research the therapist connected ongoing problems to their reports of sexual abuse while they attended St
George's School, an Anglican residential school situated near
Lytton. As a consequence of the RCMP investigation a former
dormitory supervisor at St George's was arrested and charged
with nineteen sexual offences.

An expert on sexual abuse who works at a Native alcoholism foundation in Edmonton reported that as many as 80
per cent of the Natives at church-run schools had been sexually abused. Geoffrey York comments: "Like an infectious disease, the abuse is transmitted from generation to generation.
The victims become the abusers. Research in some Canadian
Indian communities has found that seventy-five to ninety-
four percent of the residents have been sexually abused in
their childhood."[21]

The 19 October 1996 Saturday edition of the *Toronto Globe
and Mail* was headlined: "Hundreds of Cree and Ojibwa
Children Violated." Peter Moon's article, written from Fort
Albany First Nation, Ontario, states:

After decades of sexual and physical violence against hundreds of aboriginal children, criminal charges are about to
be laid against some of the priests, brothers, nuns and lay
workers who ran a residential school in this isolated Cree
community on James Bay. From 1904 to 1973, the federal
government forced thousands of bewildered and frightened Cree and Ojibwa children into St. Anne's Residential
School operated by a Roman Catholic order. Their fear
was apparently justified. Complaints lodged by many for-

mer residents of the school included heterosexual and
homosexual rape, illegal abortions, sexual fondling, forced
masturbation and many kinds of physical violence, including whipping bare buttocks with a wire strap and using a
home-made electric chair into which children were
strapped and given jolts as punishment. The complainants
told the police that as children they were forced to eat
their own vomit and kneel in painful positions for hours
on concrete floors, were locked up overnight in unlit basements and were subjected to humiliations such as having
to stand with their underpants over their heads if the
pants had fecal stains on them. If parents objected to the
treatment of their children and tried to keep them out of
the school they were told by the missionaries that their
family and welfare cheques would not be cashed and that
local stores, most of which were run at the time by the
Hudson Bay Company, would not grant them credit."[22]

The abuse suffered by Native children has given rise to the
identification of a new psychological disorder, says Moon:
"Psychologists use the term 'residential-school syndrome' to
describe the symptoms created by loss of culture, personal
identity and self-worth that are exhibited by thousands of former residential-school victims across Canada."[23]

Understandably Native children tried to escape from residential schools. They realized they were caught up in a dangerous situation and knew their lives were in jeopardy. They
were not exaggerating. They saw what was happening to other
children. Dr P.H. Bryce, one of the Department of Indian
Affairs chief medical officers, reported a shocking death toll
from tuberculosis among the residential children. This highly
contagious disease was at epidemic levels in the schools, the

result of over-crowding and inadequate nutrition. Dr Bryce surveyed 1,537 children in fifteen schools and reported a death toll of 24 per cent. He noted that the death toll would have been even higher and would have risen to 42 per cent if the health of the children had been recorded for three years after they left the school. In their *Report on Aboriginal Peoples* the commissioners comment: "The rate varied from school to school going as high as forty-seven percent at Old Sun's on the Blackfoot reserve. Kuper Island school in British Columbia, which was not included in Dr. Bryce's sample, had a rate of forty percent over its twenty-five year history." Duncan Campbell Scott of the Department of Indian Affairs admitted: "Fifty percent of the children who passed through these schools did not live to benefit from the education which they had received therein."[24]

The trauma of those who attempted to escape from the incarceration is described in numerous harrowing accounts of Native children trying to find their way home. In winter some were found frozen to death, ill clothed to make the journey. Most escapees were apprehended and returned to the schools. On one such return journey children were roped like steers to a wagon and made to run back to the school. When confronted by officials from the Department of Indian Affairs, the school principal explained that the journey was only eight miles and the horse did not trot all the way! Punishment for attempted escapes and other infractions of the rules was extreme. There is documentary evidence that "children were frequently beaten severely with whips, rods and fists, chained and shackled, bound hand and foot and locked in closets, basements, and bathrooms, and had their heads shaved or hair closely cropped."[25]

Suicide is a way to deal with an intolerable situation. Studies in the field of suicidology indicate that even very young children turn to this extreme measure as a response to experiences they can no longer bear. Some of these very young Native residential school children did turn to suicide. The Commissioners report: "Some … children met their deaths. Other children tried to find escape in death itself. In June 1981, at Muscowequan Residential School, five or six girls between the ages of eight and ten years had tied socks and towels together and tried to hang themselves. Earlier that year, a fifteen year old girl at the school had been successful in her attempt."[26]

At a residential school principals' conference, six former students were invited to share their assessment of the system. The principals were probably stunned when at least two of the speakers seized the opportunity to be confrontational. They described the system as "an insult to human dignity." One, speaking of physical and psychological abuse, described some of the punishments levied at the Mohawk Institute at Brantford, Ontario: "I have seen Indian children having their faces rubbed in human excrement … the normal punishment for bedwetters … was to have their face rubbed in his own urine." Of those who tried to escape, the former student said: "Nearly all were caught and brought back to face the music." He described how the apprehended escapees were forced to run the gauntlet where they were "struck with anything that was at hand." He completed his testimony by saying: "I have seen boys crying in the most abject misery and pain with not a soul to care – the dignity of man!"[27]

It is questionable that the children benefited in any way from the residential school experience. Those that completed the program left without the skills that would have prepared them to enter either the working world of business or commerce or industrial occupations. Psychologically they had been seriously damaged. They were a lost generation. Their connection with their communities had been severed, but they had also lost touch with themselves. They lacked any sense of identity and well-being.

It is horrifying to think that this result may have been the whole point of the exercise. If some sick and fiendish mind had contrived to undermine and destroy a culture, the cleverest plan of attack would be to break and confuse the hearts and minds of the children. Their damaged lives would continue to send shock waves of destruction throughout the generations that followed them. And that is precisely what has happened. Consultants working for the Assembly of First Nations reported the resulting damage: "The survivors of the Indian residential school system have, in many cases continued to have their lives shaped by the experiences in these schools. Persons who attend these schools continue to struggle with their identity after years of being taught to hate themselves and their culture. The residential school led to a disruption in the transference of parenting skills from one generation to the next. Without these skills, many survivors had difficulty in raising their own children. In residential schools, they learned that adults often exert power and control through abuse. The lessons learned in childhood are often repeated in adulthood with the result that many survivors of the residential school system often inflict abuse on their own children. These children in turn use the same tools on their children."[28]

Chief Cinderina Williams of Spallumcheem supported these findings through her own observations:

Some children harboured great resentment toward their parents, grandparents and their whole community for subjecting them to the horrors of the residential schools and found they could trust no one, not even themselves, for self-betrayal was common in order to survive. They had to cheat, lie, and steal to avoid punishment, get food to eat and obtain special favours, or avoid hard labour. Later when these children returned home they were aliens. They did not speak their own language, so they could not communicate with anyone other than their own counterparts. Some looked down on their families because of their lack of English, their life styles, and some were just hostile. They formed no bonds with their families, and some couldn't survive without the regimentation they had become so accustomed to ... Many, after years of rigid discipline, when released, ran amok, created havoc with their new-found freedom and would not listen to their parents, elders or anyone else in a position of authority.[29]

Chief Williams's comments identify the residential school system as a continuing cause of disruption and violence within Native family life: "Perhaps the greatest tragedy of this background was the unemotional upbringing they had. Not being brought up in a loving, caring, sharing, nurturing environment, they did not have these skills as they are not inbred but learned through observation, participation and interaction. Consequently, when these children became parents, and most did at an early age, they had no parenting skills. They did not have the capability to show affection. They sired and bred children but were unable to relate to them at any level. This is still evident today."[30]

The commissioners point to the root of the problem: "There can be no dispute: the churches and the government did not, in any thoughtful fashion, care for the children they presumed to parent. While this is traceable to systematic problems, particularly the lack of financial resources, the persistence of those problems and the unrelieved neglect of the children can be explained only in the context of another deficit – the lack of moral resources, the abrogation of parental responsibility. The avalanche of reports on the condition of the children – hungry, malnourished, ill clothed, dying of tuberculosis, overworked – failed to move either the churches or successive governments past the point of intention and on to concerned and effective remedial action."[31]

The government, religious institutions, and likely large segments of the general population were aware of what was happening in those schools. Yet at the time no action was taken to either punish the offenders or change the conditions. There is no evidence that criminal charges were laid, or even that those responsible for abuses were dismissed from their positions, though there were demands that their employers do so. If these children had been members of the white culture, there is no question that the reaction would have been otherwise. But they were just "Indian kids"!

In a series entitled *The Circle of Healing*, shown on CBC Television on 17 January 1989, producer Roy Bonisteel commented: "One of the outspoken secrets of our society is that the rate of sexual abuse in the Native community is staggering, and much of the blame for the problem can be traced directly back to our main churches to individual priests, ministers, and nuns in the residential school system that was set up to teach the Natives our culture."[32]

Early in the twenty-first century the issue of the damage inflicted upon the students is still being debated. The *Globe and Mail* reported on 28 October 2002 that the federal government was reflecting on a settlement offer by the Anglican

Church of Canada: "If the cabinet approves the offer, the door could be open to settle about 11,000 claims by students who attended the federally mandated schools from the 1930s to the early 1970s. The schools were operated primarily by the Anglican, United and Roman Catholic churches ... Mainly it could be the model thread that unravels the whole tangled skein of the residential schools and the suits and counter-suits that have been piling up in the courts for years, alleging physical, sexual and culture abuse."[33]

In the mid-1950s the government took over from the churches the responsibility of educating Native children. Day schools were constructed on the reserves. Then the policy was changed. It was decided that Native children would attend the same provincial schools that non-Native children attended. Native leaders objected to this policy, but the government proceeded with the plan. Geoffrey York comments, "The new policy resulted partly from vague feelings of egalitarianism, but it also stemmed from a desire to assimilate Indian children into white society. The provincial school system was now perceived to be the most effective way of absorbing Indian culture into the dominant white culture."

The effects of this new policy have also been devastating. A study produced by the Manitoba Indian Brotherhood in 1971 reported that of Native children who entered school in 1951–52, only 1.9 per cent reached grade twelve. Of those who entered school in 1957–58, only 5.4 per cent reached grade twelve. Based on this study it was estimated that of students who entered school in 1967–68 only 10.8 per cent would reach grade twelve compared with an average of 90 per cent for all other Manitobans. The estimates proved to be correct.[33]

The negative bias of standard textbooks also adversely affected the Native self-image. Researchers analyzing textbooks in Ontario discovered that in social studies textbooks used in 1971, Natives were portrayed "less favourably than any other ethnic group."[34] Natives were described as being primitive, unskilled, aggressive, and hostile. When they fought and killed white people, those encounters were described as "massacres." When whites fought and killed Natives, they were described as "fights" or "battles."[35]

Manuel and Posluns indicated some of the cultural consequences of the school experience on the life of the Native child:

> Schools, because they are the most widely shared and commonly experienced institution in North America, are where racism and discrimination are most experienced. The Native child faces a cruel dilemma every time he or she goes to school. Failure to continue in school may mean that he continues the poverty and deprivation that have been forced on his parents no matter how hard-working and diligent they are. Continuing in school means creating a barrier between himself and his people. The barrier is often built of isolation for much or all of the academic year while he travels to a larger centre ... Even if the child stays at home, too much of the curriculum is unrelated to any rural life; the social studies and literature he must learn are degrading and dishonest. Most important of all, the entire structure and routine of the school represent a foreign way of life that acknowledges neither his culture nor the land from which it sprang.[36]

A study by Ted Parnell of social and economic circumstances of Canadian Natives in Alberta, published by the Alberta Human Rights and Civil Liberties Association, concluded: "Schools give the impression to native children that their people are inferior and to get anywhere they will have to conform to the dominant society. The impact is a sense of inferiority."[37]

The studies precipitated a reaction from Native groups. Native leaders demanded that their children be taught in their own schools by Native teachers. Following a long, difficult struggle, schools under the jurisdiction of Native bands were established, with impressive results. At these schools, though Native leaders required that English and French be taught so that Native children could take their place in the world of business and commerce, they also insisted that Native languages must be taught. York comments: "Language is still essential to preserve their native heritage, to promote pride in native culture, and to transfer that culture from one generation to the next. Researchers have also found that Indian children learn better if they are taught in their mother tongue."[38]

The Report of the Royal Commission on Aboriginal Peoples recognizes that significant improvements have been made in the education of Native children: "There have been many important initiatives by provincial governments and school boards to create a more positive learning environment for Aboriginal children. Aboriginal support staff have often been hired, curriculum has been reviewed to eliminate obvious racism, alternative programs have been established to assist students at risk, and Aboriginal teachers are being hired, particularly at the elementary school level. Aboriginal youth are staying in school longer. There have been gains, but these have been too modest."[39] In 1996, at the time of the publication of the Royal Commission report, there was a significant difference between non-aboriginal and aboriginal academic achievement. About twice as many non-aboriginal people had high school graduation certificates as aboriginal people, and slightly more than four times as many non-aboriginal people had university degrees than aboriginal people.

Today at least 75 per cent of Native children are taught in federal or provincial schools. The results are poor. Between 80 and 90 per cent of Native children do not complete grade twelve. In the electronic age of the early twenty-first century, education is vital if Native young people are to find a place of security and a promise for a satisfying future. As the Royal Commission report comments:

> Presenters told us that education must develop children and youth as Aboriginal citizens, linguistically and culturally competent to assume the responsibilities of their nations. Youth that emerge from school must be grounded in a strong, positive Aboriginal identity. Consistent with Aboriginal traditions education must develop the whole child, intellectually, spiritually, emotionally and physically. Current education policies fail to realize these goals. The majority of Aboriginal youth do not complete high school. They leave the school system without the requisite skills for employment, and without the language and the cultural knowledge of their people. Rather than nurturing the individual, the schooling experience typically erodes identity and self-worth. Those who continue in Canada's formal education systems told us of regular encounters with racism, racism not only in interpersonal exchanges but also through the denial of Aboriginal values, perspectives and cultures in the curriculum and the life of the institution.[40]

A significant percentage of Canada's Native population remains fundamentally illiterate. Either they cannot read or write, or they do not have sufficient literacy skills to do the most basic types of work. The school dropout rate is about 90 per cent for Natives compared to the national average of 12 per cent in all of Canada. Less than 40 per cent of Status Indians complete grade eight. Yet without an education there is little possibility of finding not only meaningful employment but employment of any kind. The unemployment rate for Natives is two to three times higher than those who are non-Native. The psychological effect of the failure to become involved in a meaningful working experience is demoralizing. Being blocked from living a useful life inevitably leads to feelings of hopelessness and helplessness and a pervading spirit of despair.

SOCIAL BREAKDOWN

When I am sober, I feel like a pygmy. When I drink, I feel like a giant.
                                                    –An Alcoholic

Although Canada has been widely recognized as one of the best countries in the world in which to live, facts from the World Health Organization show that this is far from true for Canada's Native popuation. WHO data comparing non-aboriginal and aboriginal Canadians clearly indicate major concerns:

1 Life expectancy at birth for registered Natives is about seven to eight years less than for Canadians generally. Life expectancy for aboriginal men is 67 years compared to 74 years, for non-Aboriginal men; for aboriginal women it is 74 years compared to 81 years for non-aboriginal women.
2 Part of this difference in life expectancy is explained by

high rates of infant mortality among registered Natives, about twice as high as the national average. There are also high rates of injury and accidental death among aboriginal children and adolescents. Mortality in all age groups is higher for registered Natives than for Canadians generally.

3 Infectious diseases of all kinds are more common among aboriginal people than others.

4 The incidence of life-threatening degenerative conditions such as cancer, heart, liver, and lung disease – previously uncommon in the aboriginal population – is rising.

5 Overall rates of injury, violence, and self-destructive behaviour are disturbingly high.

6 Levels of over-crowding, educational failure, unemployment, welfare dependency, conflict with the law, and incarceration all point to major imbalances in the social conditions that shape the well-being of aboriginal people.[41]

Deaths are usually classified according to what are known as the NASH categories: natural, accidental, suicide, and homicide. Suicidologist Edwin S. Shneidman argues that these categories do not sufficiently include all the dynamics related to death. He recommends that the categories be changed to non-intentional, intentional, sub-intentional. Sub-intentional death is characterized by behaviours, conscious or unconscious, that will eventually destroy the person. This type of behaviour is observed in the lives of those who have lost any sense of meaning in life. The will to live is not likely to be found where there is little reason to live. One of the behaviours related to sub-intentional death is alcoholism.

Alcoholism is prevalent among Native Canadians, yet it is uncertain how widespread the problem is. The Canadian Centre on Substance Abuse reported to the Royal Commission on Aboriginal Peoples that one in five hospital admissions for alcohol-related illness in Canada is an aboriginal admission, that alcohol psychosis occurs among aboriginal people at four times the national average rate, and that the rate of liver disease among aboriginal people is three and one half times the national average.[42] The commission received contradictory reports on levels of drinking among aboriginal people as compared to non-aboriginals. They did, however, conclude that the consumption of alcohol among aboriginal people was at the problem level.

Alcoholism may be understood in a number of ways. Alcoholics Anonymous, an international organization that has had significant success in helping alcoholics, considers alcoholism to be a disease which is incurable but treatable. It is characterized by a preoccupation with alcohol and loss of control over its consumption. The disease is chronic and progresses to more serious levels endangering physical and mental health and well-being. Alcoholics develop physical disabilities and emotional problems, losing jobs and significant relationships. Eventually they lose their lives through physical deterioration or suicide. In a book now recognized as a classic in the field of self-destructive behaviour, *Man Against Himself*, the psychiatrist Carl Menninger identifies alcoholism as a slow form of suicide.

Alcoholics Anonymous recognizes that certain individuals are born with a physiological problem related to the ingestion of alcoholic beverages. Alcoholics also have a problem with feelings of low self-worth. Their sense of self-esteem is consistently low unless they drink, and then they temporarily feel better about themselves. As the disease develops, the downward spiral continues, leaving behind a trail of destruction and loss. Medical science, psychotherapy, and education have not succeeded in alleviating the problem. Alcoholics are difficult people to help. Intervention is almost impossible. Often a complete breakdown is necessary before help will be received. Sometimes during the breaking-down process, the person will have a spiritual conversion experience of the crisis type. Many middle-aged and older alcoholics tell of having had such a religious awakening. Carl Jung, one of the greatest psychotherapists the world has known, was approached for therapy by one of the men involved in the founding of Alcoholics Anonymous. Jung told him he could not help him: only a spiritual experience would be useful. This advice is reflected in the philosophy of Alcoholics Anonymous, in which small groups of alcoholics without professional leadership follow a program known as the Twelve Steps. It has been recognized as the one shining light in the dark, despairing world of alcoholism.

For centuries it was believed that Natives did not have the same tolerance for alcoholic beverages as white persons. There is no scientific basis for this belief. The assumption was based on the view that Natives were racially and physically inferior compared to members of the white race. It was generally understood that as lesser people, like children, they could not handle "strong liquor." As recently as the early 1970s the Canadian Medical Association supported this belief. An article in the association's journal alleged that "Indians had a lower tolerance for alcohol because of special characteristics in their metabolism."[43]

Geoffrey York comments: "The myth of genetic inferiority was effectively demolished by a study published in the *New*

England Journal of Medicine in 1976. The study found no significant differences in the alcohol metabolism of Indians and whites – and it discovered no other physical traits that might affect their relative tolerance of alcohol. Most experts now admit there is no evidence that Indians are genetically susceptible to liquor. The lingering myth, in fact, may simply have been a convenient way for white society to disavow any responsibility for alcohol abuse among native people."[44]

Alcoholism was not a problem for the Native before the emergence of white culture in North America. Indeed, alcohol was virtually unknown. Consequently there did not exist any code of behaviour related to the consumption of alcoholic beverages. Alcohol was introduced by the fur traders, who offered it in return for furs. In a trade war between the Hudson Bay Company and the North West Company, liquor was used as a weapon. Peter C. Newman in his study of the Hudson Bay Company reports that Natives were given more than 900,000 litres of liquor each year – two beaver pelts in exchange for one litre of diluted brandy. Newman comments: "The unrestrained use of liquor in the Canadian fur trade ranks as one of history's more malevolent crimes against humanity ... the traders of both companies debauched a civilization leaving in their wake a dispirited people and nearly destroying a once proud culture."[45]

Today alcoholism, along with glue sniffing, is at high levels among Native people. Studies of Native culture indicate that the greater the practice of paternalism with life dependent upon the welfare cheque, and any hope of meaningful employment almost non-existent, the more that feelings of worth and value are lost for the individual. Many Native people feel beyond redemption. To get thoroughly drunk, at least for a brief period, alleviates the pain.

What used to be a well-ordered culture in which the manner and means of acceptable behaviour were taught by word and example from birth no longer exists for many Native families. The consequence is *anomie,* a state or condition characterized by the breakdown or absence of social norms and values, as in the case of uprooted people. The term accurately describes the quality of life for many who live in Native society. A word closely connected to anomie is *chaos.* The support and controls formerly known in Native life have been lost. The rules and regulations related to living together in community have been forgotten. With the loss of cohesive ties that gave structure and meaning to the culture, a crowd of unconnected and uncontrolled individuals emerged. With the loss of social cohesion, group life became chaotic, a terrifying experience for all involved. It is not surprising that under those circumstances life for many Native families is presently marked by brokenness and naked violence.

Clare Brant, a Mohawk psychiatrist, ascribes the loss of meaningful activity in particular as an experience that continues to undermine the quality of Native family life. "There is an erosion of the self-esteem in Native men by chronic unemployment, which contributes to poverty, powerlessness and anomie. Any threat to this fragile self-esteem will be vigorously defended against, usually by aggression … Indian men … unemployed and idle, are constantly humiliated by having their families being supported by the welfare system. The little work which does exist on many Native reserves, such as community health representatives, child protection workers, cleaning staff, and secretarial staff, is often awarded to women. A power struggle ensues when the Native woman is the breadwinner and the exercise of intimidation and violence may be the last resort of the downtrodden warrior."[46]

In his classic study *The Religions of Man,* philosopher Hueston Smith explains the development of community and harmony within humankind and its persistence: "Through trial and error over the generations certain behavioural patterns come to be accepted as conducive to the well-being of the tribe. No council sets out consciously to decide what values the tribe wants and what rules will promote them; the pattern emerges over centuries in which the generations feel their way toward satisfying mores and away from destructive ones. Once the pattern becomes set – and societies that fail to evolve a viable one read themselves out of existence, simply vanish from the earth – it is transmitted from generation to generation, unthinkingly, passed on the young *cum lacte,* as the Romans would say, 'with the mother's milk'."[47] But as Chief Williams has explained, that process for Native people was interrupted by removing the children from their homes and destroying that communication.

With the disruption of these vital relationships, violence is bound to follow. Huston Smith refers to the insight of social analyst Walter Lippman, who describes what happens when social cohesion breaks down: "[The art of social life] has to be transmitted from the old to the young, and the habits and the ideas must be maintained as a seamless web of memory among the bearers of the tradition, generation after generation ... When the continuity of the tradition of civility is ruptured, the community is threatened. Unless the rupture is repaired, the community will break down into factional ... wars."[48] For Native people, what has erupted is war within the family. Violence within Native families is widespread. *The Report of the Royal Commission on Aboriginal Peoples* has a special section headed "Family Violence." The commissioners report: "Aboriginal people perceive that the family as an institution is under severe stress from internal violence, which is both a symptom of stress and a cause of further distress. This message was communicated most powerfully by Aboriginal women and their organizations in our hearings, although men and young people expressed concern as well."[49]

The commissioners note that violence is not restricted to one or two families but is experienced throughout the life of the whole community. They relate the cause to government interventions that have disturbed community and family living, observing that "violence within Aboriginal communities is fostered and sustained by a racist social environment that promulgates demeaning stereotypes of Aboriginal men and women and seeks to diminish their value as human beings and their right to be treated with dignity."[50]

When the experience of social cohesion was not passed from generation to generation within the Native community, a vacuum developed. This created an environment marked by confusion and uncertainty, giving opportunity for anger and violence to fester. One witness who appeared before the commission shared an example in which social cohesion was replaced by abuse that was passed from one generation to the next. The process had its beginning in a residential school: "One good example is my grandpa. His education was up to grade two, I think. From what my father tells me, there was a lot of abuse going on. A lot of name-calling, a lot of put-downs with the priest and the kids. For every little thing they got the whip. My grandpa grew up with that and he learned that, then he used it on his kids. Then my father used it on us. If I don't try to do something about it, I'm going to use it on my kids. So that's the pattern, where we picked it up from the boarding school."[51]

Anger and anxiety are effects rather than causes. The presence of anomie demonstrates the loss of structure in everyday life. Meaning, purpose, direction – the existential dynamics that support the reasons for living – are no longer evident. In their stead is chaos, which gives rise to the emergence of the primary negative emotion – fear. It is fear that gives birth to the other two negative emotions. The first of these is a form of free-floating anxiety related to issues of survival. The second is anger, a surging negative reaction to the unfairness and uncertainty of life and living. The legacy of fear lies beneath the variety of despairing responses that Natives express, as they experience the deterioration of a way of life they loved and depended upon for generations. It is understandable that anger and violence have erupted within an atmosphere of fear which threatens to engulf and finally destroy the Native people.

Benjamin Chee Chee was born into such an environment. To be a Native in Canadian society was a terrible inheritance. Born into a culture dominated by the white race, he received before long the message familiar to most Natives: You are not wanted!

Frederick Brown has said that Chee Chee hated white people. It would have been surprising had he felt differently. Native people have little reason to trust and respect the white race. Although Chee Chee appeared warm, congenial, and accepting at times, his public persona was quickly brushed aside when he was drunk. He then expressed a powerful, consuming hatred. He had much to be angry about. Fate had robbed him of a father at the beginning of his life's journey, and he was soon to lose his mother. For most of his life he lived in poverty. He experienced failure in school and in relationships. He was generally unemployed or worked at menial tasks. Racial harassment, numerous conflicts with the law, and incarceration in jails and prisons were part of his day-by-day existence. The unrelenting disease of alcoholism continued to exercise its deteriorating influence.

Chee Chee's tragic history has been repeated countless times among young Natives. Some succeed in finding their way to a creative life experience. With them lies hope for the future of the aboriginal people. But many young Natives experience extreme problems and lack the capacity to deal with them. Most of their lives are lived in fractured communities. Consequently, they lack the strength, the skills, and the will to endure. A significant number cannot see any pathway that will lead them to a full and satisfying life. Weakened by depression, influenced by the self-destructive behaviour of other Natives, they see only one possibility.

6

THE ACT OF SUICIDE

Suicide is not a crisis of identity. It is a crisis of locus.
It is not who you are but where you are at in your life.
                                    –Edwin S. Shneidman, suicidologist

To fully comprehend the death of Benjamin Chee Chee it is
necessary to understand the extent of self-destructive
behaviour among young Canadian Natives and the reasons
why they kill themselves. When the Royal Commission on
Aboriginal Peoples issued the report of their findings in
1996, the commissioners felt compelled to address some
concerns immediately. One problem stood out as being particularly urgent – the act of suicide: "Too many Aboriginal
youth and young adults are pointing shotguns at their
heads, putting ropes around their necks, destroying their
powers of reason with the fumes of gasoline and glue. Even
one such death or serious injury would be too many. It is
hard to imagine a public responsibility more pressing than
to stop them."[1] The demographics of self-destructive behaviour ranks the suicide of young Canadian Natives at one of
the highest levels in the world.

In most countries, adolescents and young adults commit
suicide the least, and the middle-aged and the elderly the
most. Canada is one of the few exceptions to this pattern

among countries that record and report incidents of self-destructive behaviour. For non-aboriginals in Canada the lowest numbers of suicides involve young people, the highest numbers the middle-aged and the elderly. For aboriginal Canadians the highest rate of suicide occurs with males and females between the ages fifteen and twenty-five years of age.

A Native health liaison worker describes a typical situation:

For the past four years, most of my time has been spent on dealing with crisis situations brought on by suicides and attempted suicides of youth within Shibogama communities. My work has not been easy. It is difficult to attend funerals of young people that have taken their lives with their own hands. It is often overwhelming and painful to comfort a parent, a friend, a grandparent or the community members as a whole when a sudden and shocking tragedy such as the death of a young person occurs. This is the reality of working in the field of suicide prevention ... Shibogama First Nations have suffered the loss of 11 young lives since 1987. The method used by the youth to take their lives in the Shibogama area is by hanging using whatever is available at the moment of complete despair. Within the Shibogama communities alone there were 135 reported suicide attempts between 1987 and 1991. In 1992, Kingfisher Lake reported another 22 attempts between January and August. Altogether we had 157 attempts in the four communities. The methods used in attempted suicides are either by hanging or by overdose. Many other attempted suicides have not been reported and are not recorded. Most of the victims of suicide and attempted suicides range in the age group of 14 to 25 years of age. Most of the victims are males, single

and unemployed ... Most of [them] never received proper counselling due to lack of resources.[2]

A teacher reported to the Royal Commission: "Suicide is a
major problem among Aboriginal youth. Racism, loss of culture, physical and mental abuse, family discord, feelings of
boredom, loneliness and powerlessness all contribute to the
personal pain that leads these young people to choose suicide.
Drug and alcohol abuse tends to exaggerate the problem.
'Suicide relieves the pain,' as one student said. And another:
'Suicide has crossed everyone's mind once or twice.'"[3]

The material that follows should give the reader some sense
of what has gone on for many years with regard to the act of
suicide among young aboriginals. Two studies, the first from
the mid-1970s, the other the Nishnawbe Aski Youth Forum
on Suicide held near the end of the 1990s, establish that there
has been little change in the level of suicide in a quarter of
century.

In the fall of 1976 and spring of 1977 I participated in an
investigation of the suicide epidemic on the Wikwemikong
Indian reserve on Manitoulin Island in Northern Ontario. I
was associated with John A. Ward, director of psychiatry at
the Algoma Sanatorium in Sudbury, and Joseph Fox, a Native
social counsellor. Dr Ward and I presented papers analyzing
the epidemic at the International Congress on Suicide
Prevention and Crisis Intervention in Helsinki in June 1977.

Dr Ward, with Joseph Fox and a team of investigators
including several members of the Native community, had
interviewed families and neighbours of the suicide victims
and obtained information from the police, the coroner's
office, hospital administration records, and probation and
correction reports. My study focused on the state of being of

Native culture and the way in which those circumstances contributed to the large number of suicides among young Natives
throughout Canada. These studies, the first on the suicide of
Canadian Natives to be presented in a global forum, were
published in the congress proceedings. What follows is based
on the reports of Dr Ward and his colleagues.

On Christmas Day in 1974 a seventeen-year-old youth and
his sister were alone in a farmhouse in the isolated community of Kaboni on Manitoulin Island. They were members of a
family whose familial relationships were marked by fighting
and tension. The parents quarrelled constantly, and their relationship had deteriorated to the point that the mother
planned to leave and move in with a daughter who lived in
Toronto. The young man paced the floor while he drank thirteen ounces of vodka. He told his sister he was going to kill
himself. She did not take him seriously. He went into a bedroom, loaded a small rifle and shot himself in the forehead.
Eight hours later he died.

This death was the first of a series of eight suicides occurring in a rural community of thirty-seven families, part of a
large Ojibway Native reserve of some 3,000 men, women, and
children on Manitoulin Island. The suicides occurred in the
space of a twelve-month period from December 1974 to
November 1975. The magnitude of the suicide rate, and the
limits of time and geographical space, placed the deaths in the
category of an epidemic.

The eight Native victims ranged in age from seventeen to
thirty-one years with a median age of twenty-two years. They
included five males and three females. All were single. Six
used firearms as the mode of suicide, shooting themselves
through the head with .22 calibre rifles. One hung himself in
a barn, and the other victim died of an overdose of chlorpro-

mazine and hypnotics. The three females all shot themselves through the head with .22 calibre rifles.

Alcohol ingestion was confirmed in three of the cases by blood alcohol analysis and was evident in the reports received on three others. In only one case was it clear that the victim had not consumed any alcohol in the period immediately prior to the suicide.

All of these young people gave a warning of their intent. Some of the warnings were unclear and could easily have been misunderstood or ignored. Only one wrote a suicide note. She wrote two letters to friends and a third letter to a lover who later proved to be non-existent. She also left a message to whoever found her. It was written on her leg: "I hate myself – true."

Six of the suicides occurred in or on the property of the parental home. One occurred at a sister's home, the victim having recently been evicted from his parents' home. The other suicide, of a female who worked as a housekeeper, occurred in front of the home of her employer. Three of the victims had suffered the loss of a parent, while in two other families a parent had been severely ill for a long time.

Three of the families had a history of violent death prior to the suicide epidemic: a suicide, a car accident while intoxicated, and a collision with a train, also while intoxicated. In another family a younger sister had attempted suicide two weeks before the suicide of the victim. In still another family a sister had attempted suicide by overdose prior to the suicides of her two brothers. The victims were neither the youngest nor the oldest of the siblings. All were members of large families of five to twelve children.

Each of the suicide victims had attained some secondary school education. Only one seemed to be able to cope with school. He had completed high school and attained an additional certificate in office practice. The others either dropped out of school or were expelled. Two of the male victims had spent time in the correctional school system. The educational level achieved by the victims, however, was similar to other students from the reserve. While nearly all completed elementary school, the majority dropped out of school at the grade nine level.

None of the victims seemed to be able to keep steady employment. Three had worked in timber operations on a seasonal basis and in occasional jobs in southern Ontario. Of the three female victims one had worked in Toronto and Chicago but returned to the reserve to care for an invalid mother, while another did housekeeping work with a family.

The eight individuals in this group had one characteristic in common. They were isolates; they lived within themselves. They had neither the compulsion nor the ability to initiate, develop or sustain close, meaningful relationships. None had a lover at the time of the suicide. Two teenage males were reported to have no interest in girls, although one had a superficial relationship with a girl at one time. Of the other three males, one had a childhood sweetheart, but she had married someone else. One complained that he could never keep a girlfriend, and the other had no intimate relationships with anyone. Two of the females had not had lovers. Only one member of the group had close friendships, and they were her Alcoholics Anonymous sponsors.

Their physical health was adequate, but their emotional well-being was unstable. Two of the victims had been admitted to psychiatric facilities. One of them had several psychiatric admissions following a depressed fracture of the skull requiring bone grafting. Another victim, a female, had repeated admissions to a mental hospital as well as several arrests for "acting-out" behaviour.

The victims were all vulnerable individuals with negative self-esteem. The young Native with the bone graft was called "Copper Head" or "Brass Head" by his peers. Another victim reluctantly wore a wig in public because of a loss of hair. Their personalities were marked since childhood by inability to develop intimacy in interpersonal relationships. They did not find satisfaction in family relationships and lacked the social skills to relate to others outside the parental family. They tended to communicate with family members in a superficial way and were not able to directly express their feelings in the face of conflict. Although Natives are inclined to internalize feelings, this group carried the tendency to the extreme.

Although unable to relate well to their families, the victims were overly dependent on them for interpersonal and social needs. They were thus extremely vulnerable to stresses that occurred within the parental family. The inevitable loss of members through marriage, employment, or death would deepen these feelings of distress and of being deserted. Breakdown in the marital relationship occurred in five of the families. Family discord was present and constant in all of them.

Conflict with one of the parents, especially the natural father, was common. So was the use of derogatory remarks levelled at the suicide victim by the family members. There was a heavy use of alcohol in all but one family. In four of the families the father drank excessively. The mother of one of the victims was an alcoholic and had drowned while intoxicated in a water-filled ditch. In two other cases both parents were recorded as heavy drinkers. Many of the siblings of the suicide victims also had drinking problems. The family drinking brought about violent reactions and smouldering quarrels, resulting in withdrawal, isolation, and loss of self-esteem.

Immediately prior to the suicidal act, family conflict was present and was regarded as a precipitating event. At that time the victims experienced the loss of support from a significant family member. The decision to commit suicide was catalyzed by alcohol ingestion and lack of response to cries for help. The victims had ideated about their intention to kill themselves. Since most had clearly planned the act for some time, there appeared to be little impulsivity involved. They generally attempted to cope with stress by using escape, withdrawal, denial, internalization, and alcohol. These mechanisms were self-defeating, isolating them further and making their lives hopeless and meaningless.

The process of acculturation – that is, the powerful influences at work to cause aboriginal people to become alienated from their own culture and to adopt the industrial, technological white culture – had proceeded in this reserve to a greater degree than on many others in Northern Ontario. The close proximity to industrial society was likely a central cause for this rapid rate of acculturation. The process had lowered the perceived value of the traditional Native heritage , inducing a negative image of being Native. A backlash on the reserve had recently occurred with a demand to return to traditional values. This had resulted in considerable social upheaval and community splitting. Although those of the older age group remained loyal to their ancestral values, many of the middle-aged were drawn to the lifestyle of white society. Some young people sided with their grandparents; others did not. It was a confusing and difficult period.

Those young people who had left the reserve to work in other parts of Canada and the USA, intrigued by the white culture's values and lifestyle, soon discovered they were unwelcome and had no place in white society. Identified as "Indian" and categorized as second-class citizens, they lacked the ability or the will to cope. They had returned to the reserve with expectations, only to find it empty, meaningless, and disappointing. Life on the reserve was a bare existence marked by family dispute and alcohol abuse and without promise of meaningful employment. They were alone in this dismal situation without the capacity to develop significant relationships. They did not belong to a family system where they could discover an identity or the experience of belonging. They did not revere their culture, and they were not wanted elsewhere. They were trapped. To whom could they turn for help and guidance? At one time there were the aboriginal elders. But these were either not available or the young Natives had lost respect for them, experiencing them as just another group of old people who had also lost their way.

Loss of helping resources had created a vacuum. Social gatherings that had formerly been a significant community experience had lost their meaning and were now marked by alcohol abuse. Consequently a state of anomie developed. A loss of social norms and values rendered the community empty and rootless. Lives were lived in a state of detachment and confusion. The ensuing instability led to disaster. Rates of suicide and homicide and the incidence of accidents and violent death all became excessively high. Alcohol played a significant role. Car accidents and misuse of firearms took their toll. The rate of violent deaths on the Wikwemikong Reserve doubled within a decade. The setting was ripe for a suicide epidemic.

Dr Ward refuted media attempts to blame the deaths on a "religious cult":

Press reports of the suicide epidemic focussed on the idea that the suicides were induced by the presence of a malignant influence imposed by curses put on by someone trained in the ways of the Indian religious cult. This curse was known as the "bear walk." No evidence is available to show that such ideas were present in any but one of the victims and this was the "post-hoc" explanation of the accidental death of another brother. Whether one speculates on the presence of a malignant "bear-walker" or holds to the theory of "contagion," a malignant atmosphere existed – an atmosphere that offered no hope of a meaningful future to its youth and indeed only loss, as the only social group with whom they could relate was breaking up, as family members died or left to get married or find jobs. The tranquillizing and stupefying effects of alcohol failed. A malignant spirit existed in that community and needed to be exorcised by community action.[4]

By "contagion" Dr Ward was making reference to a significant characteristic noted in the dynamics of suicidal behaviour. Suicide may be understood as a learned, problem-solving manoeuvre. Compliant, confused, rootless individuals tend to be influenced by the behaviour of others. In an environment that has been contaminated by suicide ideation, attempted suicide, and the completed act of suicide, the expectation of suicidal activity is to be anticipated.

More than twenty years have passed since the epidemic. During that period a creative response has been made. The deeply shaken Native community took action that included public education with the intent of developing understanding about alcohol abuse and suicidal behaviour. The nurturing of a sense of community was necessary in the initial phase to respond to feelings of grief and guilt that swept through the families. The rebirth of a community that could recover social norms and values and work together was also essential for mutual support, well-being, and healing. Understandably the epidemic created fears that all would become engulfed by self-destructive behaviour. People were driven to come together to find their way out of the dilemma.

The community was forced to turn to its own inner resources to survive. Members were introduced to measures they could use to respond creatively in a crisis situation. Community awareness was renewed and a willingness to respond developed. The sense that they belonged and were responsible for each other was created and nurtured. Along with this community movement, Dr Ward was instrumental in establishing a counselling centre for one-to-one therapy and family counselling.

Transformation could not and did not happen overnight. It would take generations to re-establish a community. But they began the journey. The Royal Commission on Aboriginal Peoples reports on the progress made some twenty-five years following the epidemic:

> The community-based programs at Wikwemikong have not completely rooted out the distress that puts young people at risk. In the words of one caregiver, "the threat of suicide is always with us." A recent survey of children and youth in the local elementary and high schools revealed that 25 per cent felt worried or depressed most or all of the time. About 35 per cent said that there was rarely anyone for them to talk to when they felt "down." About 20 per cent said that when they felt down they thought about hurting themselves. Adolescents still represent a big

portion of the caseload at the Nadmadwin Mental Health
Clinic ... Although problems have not disappeared, com-
munity-based mental health programs have clearly
helped. In 1993, there was one suicide and about ten
attempts in the Manitoulin-North Shore catchment area.
The manager of the Nadmadwin Clinic attributes the current level of psychological stability at Wikwemikong to
two things: the success of public education to build
awareness and collective responsibility for mental health
and wellness, so that personal, family and social problems
are usually referred for help before they become severe;
and community development more generally, such that
programs for collective self-care are much better developed in Wikwemikong today than they were 20 years ago
when eight young people chose to die in one year.[5]

The history of the aboriginal people records that the act of
suicide was once a rarity. In communities where the individual is respected and esteemed, where one belongs and is
accepted unconditionally, suicide is almost unknown. That is
clearly not the situation today. The Royal Commission noted
that a significant change had taken place: "The pattern of
meaning of suicide among Aboriginal people appears to have
undergone a disturbing transformation over time. In the
past, those few suicides that occurred were primarily acts of
the old or the ill. Their deaths were acts of self-sacrifice, spar-
ing others the burden of extra care. Although they brought
sadness and loss, these deaths were also a profound affirma-
tion of life and of the importance of group survival. In contrast, Aboriginal suicide today is more likely to be an act of
the young, an expression of hopelessness by those on the
brink of life. As such, it is a negation of the future and deeply
demoralizing to Aboriginal people."[6]

The central dynamic that drives young people to kill themselves is a sense of rootlessness. Edwin Shneidman has commented: "Suicide is not a crisis of identity, it is a crisis of locus; it is not who you are but where you are at in your life." An overview of the lives of the young Natives who have killed themselves reveals that they had no place to be. There was no one for them, nor could they allow others to become close to them. Their growth as human beings had been stunted. They did not learn to open themselves to others. Dr Ward characterized the victims of the suicide epidemic as isolates. Though they might have had superficial social skills with respect to the development of intimacy, their personalities were impenetrable. Their shield was mistrust. Perhaps they had tried closeness once and in the process become badly burned. Lord Sainsbury, a researcher in the field of suicide research in Britain, points to a basic flaw in the personalities of those who take their lives: "Loneliness may be a factor, but a close examination shows their life history is the end product of a long history of inability to relate satisfactorily to others." Isaac Sakinofsky, a psychiatrist and well-known Canadian researcher in the field of suicidology, in a workshop for suicidologists described the characteristics of young people who kill themselves: "They come from disadvantaged, horrendous family backgrounds. They grow up to be depressed people, with poor self-esteem and, rankling with resentment, they move from crisis to crisis in their lives."

Suicide for the young is the end of a long fruitless search for an answer to a life that has been an enigma. Although there are always exceptions, the list of characteristics describing the life and times of a young person who has committed suicide are constant: an isolate; uncomfortable with members of the opposite gender; school/work problems; drug/alcohol abuse; suicide attempts; depressive moods; aggressive behaviour; low frustration tolerance; deepening feelings of despair; parental conflict; alcoholism within the family; absentee father; existential anxiety reflected in lack of purpose, meaning, or direction.

Audra Pambrun, an American Blackfoot Native, has studied suicide among members of the Blackfoot nation, a tribe of of Algonquin stock whose traditional territory spans the Canada –u.s. border. Pambrun's article, "Suicide, Homicide and Alcoholism Among American Indians," notes typical social characteristics of the Native who has committed suicide:

> He is a male between 15 and 24 years of age.
> He is single.
> He is under the influence of alcohol just before the suicide attempt.
> He has lived with a number of ineffective or inappropriate parental substitutes because of family disruption.
> He has spent time in boarding schools and has been moved from one to another.
> He has been raised by caretakers who have come in conflict with the law.
> He has often been jailed at an early age.
> He has experienced an emotional loss, such as divorce, desertion, or death in the family.
> He has experienced a past loss through violence of someone to whom he felt attached.[7]

Pambrun compiled that list over twenty-five years ago. If one were to develop such a list today, it would remain much the same, though not all the victims, of course, are male.

Characteristics describing the personalities and lifestyles of young white people who commit suicide are similar to those of young Natives. However, one major difference stands out: in terms of ratio of the general population far greater numbers of young Natives kill themselves than young white people. Why? The answer is found in the phenomenon of cultural conflict, a life experience affecting all aboriginals. This conflict results in a deadly loss of cultural identity. Saul Levine, a Canadian psychiatrist, has said: "When values come into question, when leaders are no longer followed, when there are no predictable customs and rituals – then all the indices of disintegration take place – alcoholism, drugs, suicide."[8]

We have been conditioned to believe that there are inherent differences among the peoples of this earth which will determine cultural and individual achievements. This conditioning has led white Canadians to believe that the white race is superior to all others – an attitude of racism or bigotry most of us would deny holding. Often we are unaware of the dark side of our psyches. Fortunately, as we become immersed in a multicultural society and encounter men, women, and children from cultures other than our own, we do learn how much we are alike.

Unfortunately, for many who have belonged to cultures other than white culture, contact with white society has in the past not been useful or enriching. Indeed, for many aboriginal people in Canada, life with white society has been a ruinous experience. The wounds that have been inflicted are deep and not easily healed. Such wounds are passed on, affecting generation after generation.

The instrument that initially inflicted the wounds was called "assimilation," a term with similar meaning to that of acculturation.[9] Our forebears considered aboriginal culture inferior to their own, and as such, it had to go. Assimilation was the intent. It failed. Hundreds of years and billions of dollars later, Canada is still trying to assimilate – and to save – its aboriginals. Aboriginal people themselves remain adamant: they will not be absorbed. The tragedy is that in the conflict many have been fatally wounded. Though they have not been absorbed into another culture, they have lost something of inestimable value. They have lost touch with their own culture.

Just as warmth, sunshine, food, and oxygen are essential for life, so is culture. Edward Tylor, a nineteenth century anthropologist, described culture as that complex whole which includes knowledge, belief, art, morals, law, customs, and any other capabilities and habits acquired by the individual as a member of society. Tylor equated culture with civilization. Culture includes the total life of the environment, including all material and non-material products of the group's life, a product that is handed down from one generation to another.

A culture may be likened to a household. The physical structure in which the extended family lives is an environment furnished with comfortable and familiar things. Several generations abide in this dwelling, perhaps with a variety of animal friends considered to be members of the family. Smells, odours, and tastes, invisible to the eye but ever present, send forth an at-home feeling. Foods that sustain and satisfy physical needs are prepared and served with care and love. Members of the family, though individually different, have a similar physical appearance that identifies them as belonging to the household. Within that environment there is a communal bond that communicates the feeling of love and security. Between all members of the household an expectation exists that a standard of behaviour is practised not only between themselves but also with those they come into contact with outside. This understanding of how humans relate to one another is taught through instruction and personal modelling. Knowledge about the Creator and creation and the incorporation of spiritual values into the daily affairs of life are passed from generation to generation as guidelines directing each member of the family towards a full life experience. The household is strong, stable, and deep rooted. Its members are prepared to go out into the world to interact with others without losing sight of who they are and where they belong.

From that perspective a culture may be seen as more than a way of life: it is life itself. Culture is who we are. If we lose our culture, we lose our life, for culture presents us with many gifts, foremost among them being existential reasons for living. Culture gives us purpose, meaning, and direction. The following comment by a young Native teenager poignantly conveys a deep sense of loss of culture: "I have a grandfather who is 80 years old and I have been growing up with him for my 18 years. I cannot speak my language. I try. But I love him more than anything, and there's communication there … you can feel the love between us and I can rub his hand and we know we understand each other. But there is something missing when we cannot listen to the stories they have to tell, or explain how you are feeling about something. And it's very frustrating for me, knowing that this very important part of my culture is being lost."[10]

Many other young Natives have moved away from the source of their culture, the elders, the "living libraries". In a frantic search for a meaningful existence, many aboriginal people have migrated to large urban centres with the hope that somehow things will finally work out for them. Some have found a satisfying life experience. But this group is a small minority. Generally, migration to the city has turned out to be disappointing. Poor living conditions, high unem-

ployment, racism, and life on welfare have led to deep confusion and dismay. In their experience of lostness, many turn to
alcohol or drugs. Such a lifestyle may be described as a slow
form of suicide.

The *Report of the Royal Commission on Aboriginal Peoples*
underlines a real concern over the migration of young Natives
to urban society. Almost half of all aboriginal people under
the age of twenty-five live in non-reserve urban centres. While
some have been born there, most have come searching for a
fulfilling life experience. The majority live in urban areas with
populations of more than 100,000 – Montreal, Toronto,
Winnipeg, Saskatoon, Edmonton, and Vancouver. The commission expresses both concern and understanding for these
young Natives:

> Urban youth do not want to be seen as traitors to their
> home communities. Many have a deep commitment to
> helping strengthen and enrich their communities. In
> some cases, they would stay if the community offered
> them the opportunities they seek. But to gain the neces-
> sary skills and resources – through education, work, and
> health care – they sometimes have to move to an urban
> environment for at least a few years. For some, the city
> becomes their community. Once in the city, they find new
> pressures and challenges. Substance abuse is one of the
> most pervasive problems facing Aboriginal youth. Like
> the high rates of incarceration, however, substance abuse
> is symptomatic of a deeper malaise: loss of identity and
> low self-esteem. In urban centres these feelings can be
> amplified if there is no readily apparent Aboriginal
> community to turn to for support.[11]

An epigraph in Margaret Laurence's *The Diviners* describes the ideal support, the living connection, in which those who go ahead leave a path for those who follow: "But they had their being once and left a place to stand on."[12] Erik Erikson, in his life-stage theory, identifies the process of contributing a sense of meaning and direction to the next generation as *generativity*. It an important life task of the elder and a vital characteristic of any living culture. For young Natives who kill themselves, there is no "place to stand on." Deprived of their culture, they have been left no legacy.

Among the ever-growing number of young Natives who have killed themselves was Benjamin Chee Chee. He destroyed himself at the very moment when he was breaking through to an even higher level in his creative life. His death continues to be perplexing. From one perspective it is obvious that he was on a course of self-destruction. From another point of view his future was filled with optimism and realized hope. Norwegian suicidologist Nils Retterstol indicates a defining moment in the life of the suicidal person in which that person has a wish to die and a wish to live, both at the same time. This intrapsychic conflict precisely marked the struggle within Chee Chee's life. We turn now to explore the inner struggle that engulfed him and ended his existence.

7

THE SUICIDE OF
BENJAMIN CHEE CHEE

The most difficult thing a man has to do is protect himself
against himself. —Professor Erwin Stengel

Benjamin Chee Chee was born on 26 March 1944. He died at
the Ottawa General Hospital at 3:10 A.M., 14 March 1977,
twelve days before his thirty-third birthday. His death was
the result of a suicide attempt in the Ottawa City Jail. The
medical report reveals that he died of anoxia, an abnormally
low amount of oxygen in the body tissues.

Chee Chee strangled himself with an apparatus fashioned
by his own hand. He stripped off his shirt and used it as a
rope. He tied one end around his throat, the other to the cell
bars. Then he slumped down on his haunches. The shirt fab-
ric tightened, constricting his windpipe so that he was unable
to breathe. He could have regained the ability to breathe by
rising to his feet. He refused to stop the choking. His determination was to destroy himself. Unyielding, he continued to
slump, tightening the shirt around his throat. Within minutes
he lost consciousness. But he was still alive. Approximately
fifty-three hours would pass before he would be declared
brain dead.

The jail guard checking the cell block found him crumpled
unconscious on the floor. He was immediately rushed to

Emergency at the Ottawa General Hospital. The struggle to save his life began. It was too late. The physician told Frederick Brown that if Chee Chee had survived, he would probably have been severely brain damaged. The artist had been destroyed.

Chee Chee's chosen method of suicide is a metaphor graphically illustrating the destructive dynamics at work throughout his life. For years he had been ensnared by the disease of alcoholism, a progressive destructive force. Everything that the alcoholic has will be lost – family, friends, material possessions, vocation, self-respect, physical and emotional health, and finally life itself. All worthwhile connections will be destroyed. Eventually the alcoholic will choke himself off from all sources of well-being.

Alcoholism was not the underlying cause that led Chee Chee to kill himself. Throughout his life he had been engaged in a desperate struggle related to uncertainty about his identity and where he belonged. He was a lost, confused soul. At times a part of his personality would break through into a life that seemed meaningful and satisfying. Then another part would drag him down again. The theme of his inner scenario was to fail.

Edwin Shneidman has observed, "The common cognitive state in suicide is constriction."[1] The effect of this constriction is a "tunnelling" of perspective, a common feature noted in those resolved to end their lives. They have reached the point where they have no place to turn. They are bankrupt, bereft of supportive resources. They scan their life experience and become convinced that anything or anyone they have been able to turn to for succour in the past is no longer there for them. No one cares, understands, or is concerned. They no longer have the capacity to range through a number of

options, contemplating each one, to finally make a decision to
select the one that will free them from the present dilemma.
For them no option remains except death.

The process of counselling suicidally inclined persons is
to introduce them to a number of options. This technique
enables them to broaden their vision, to widen the constricting perspective, to prevent the development of tunnel vision.
If the psychotherapy is successful, they will be able to perceive
five or six options instead of one. But for the person stub-
bornly committed to the resolution of self-murder, the nar-
rowing has become complete. So it was for Chee Chee. I asked
the Native artist Hugh McKenzie if he was surprised when he
received news that his lifelong friend had killed himself. He
immediately responded, "No, he talked about suicide all the
time." Suicide for Chee Chee was always the option if life
became impossible.

Shneidman quotes Boris Pasternak's description of the suicidal deaths of several young Russian poets, underlining the
constriction that put their lives in peril: "A man who decides
to commit suicide puts a full stop to being, he turns his back
on his past, he declares himself to be bankrupt and his memories to be unreal. They can no longer help or save him, he has
put himself beyond their reach. The continuity of his inner
life is broken, and his personality is at an end. And perhaps
what finally makes him kill himself is not the firmness of his
resolve but the unbearable quality of anguish which belongs
to no one, of this suffering in the absence of the sufferer, of
this waiting which is empty because life has stopped and no
one can feel it."[2]

Chee Chee had reached this level of constriction. He
believed that he alone could feel his terrible anguish. No one
beside himself could experience the agonizing dilemma of his
life. It was a knot which he could not untie, despite his strong

desire to be free. He was engaged in an intrapersonal combat in which he always lost. Remorse was his constant companion. He was back where he had been so many times before – a dirty, disgusting, "drunken Indian" on the floor of a jail cell. The "'celebrated artist" looked upon the scene with loathing. Chee Chee hated and despised what he believed he really was. His life had been a cruel joke. He could no longer tolerate the constant slipping back into the past. Only one option was left.

Shneidman identifies the decision to leave the impossible, chaotic present as egression, the act of leaving. An individual may egress from an occupation, from a relationship, indeed from any situation. The act of suicide is the ultimate egression – a total, absolute departure. Chee Chee chose to depart from life because it was too painful. A woman who committed suicide left a note describing her painful existence as if "an emotional spear" had been thrust into her belly. Egression from life offers the certainty of peace and freedom from unendurable suffering and intolerable anguish. Those who choose to leave life by their own hand do not do so because they choose death. They leave because they can no longer stand the pain of their existence. Psychiatrist Dr Casriel comments: "It isn't that he feels he would be happier dead, just that there would be less pain." In a suicide note addressed to her therapist, an adolescent girl declared, "Suicide is like mercy killing. People pull plugs on people to put them out of their misery. I want to be put out of misery but no one will do it for me so I have to do it myself. When you look at it, it seems so logical."[3]

Suicide for Chee Chee was the termination of a long process. He had lived a life marked by instability. He had lost his family and his culture. He was restless and spiritually hungry, constantly in search of some experience that would bring meaning and purpose to his life. He was tormented and rootless. He did not have a permanent home, his last address was a hotel. His sense of worth and value as a human being was labile. Within hours his mood could change from mania to deepest gloom and depression. While he developed a few close, intimate relationships, these connections were always tenuous. He would not allow genuine closeness. He had learned that intimacy was painful and dangerous. He was a loner. That was his choice.

His painting of a group of bison together facing one way with one facing in the opposite direction was a graphic description of life on Chee Chee's terms. The paradox of his lifestyle indicated that he was always searching for intimacy, yet he was most comfortable when he was cut off from others. Solitude was safer. Rejecting others before they could reject him was his way of dealing with the fear of alienation.

Although these negative characteristics are strong indicators of the possibility of self-destructive behaviour, their presence does not mean that a suicide will occur. Two additional factors must be involved: feelings of hopelessness and helplessness – characteristics that add up to the sense of despair. Hopelessness and helplessness saturated Chee Chee's being as he lay on the floor of that jail cell. Those emotions triggered the action to end his life. Hopelessness had visited him many, many times before. Layer upon layer of hopelessness continued to build until it finally broke him. Towards the end of his life he was drinking uncontrollably, trying to quiet the inner voice telling him that there was no hope of change, that the only way out was self-destruction. The presence of despair emphasized that there was only one answer to this existential problem. There was no help available that would one more time strengthen and guide the way to healing, health, and freedom.

The experience of despair is the convincing element, the

compelling inner voice, that fires the suicidal ideation and leads to the act of suicide. Despair is the most seductive of emotions. It is a subtle sensation that can lead to disaster without the individual being aware of what he is doing to himself. Erwin Stengel comments: "The most difficult thing a man has to do is to protect himself against himself." This statement could be applied to many areas of life experience, but in particular it applies to the suicidal person.

Benjamin Chee Chee was his own deadly enemy. There were clearly two parts of his personality. One part was warm, friendly, apparently happy, generous with money and possessions. He was caring and supportive of his friends. He searched for and found his mother, and cared for her. The other side of his personality was vicious, angry, and violent, particularly when intoxicated, subject to depression and mood swings.

Frederick Brown described a meeting with Chee Chee just days before Chee Chee's suicide in which the dark side of his personality was revealed. Brown is a wise and discerning human being who had known Chee Chee for years and was likely his closest confidante. On that occasion he saw a different man. Although he had seen him in personal torment, he had never seen Chee Chee with such a complete loss of self-esteem and feelings of personal loathing and rejection. Chee Chee spoke openly about his acute feelings of despair and isolation, describing a life filled with darkness and pain. Nearly twenty years after that meeting, Brown still felt the anguish of listening to Chee Chee describe his torturous life journey.

This exposure of a desperate inner experience of worthlessness was in sharp contrast to Chee Chee's current public life. His work had met with approval and recognition on a national scale, as well as material rewards. The possibility of international recognition was developing. All these wonderful events were happening in the present, yet Chee Chee was sinking into a pit of despair. The fluctuations of his sense of well-being were a reflection of his fragility. A fault line running through him marked the vulnerability that had always been at the core of his personality. The issue was never whether or not he would destroy himself, but when. The spark that set off the suicidal reaction was anger, an integral part of his personality. His angry, violent emotions were at times expressed in volcano-like eruptions. It took a number of police officers to subdue him when they were attempting to arrest him. Chee Chee was the aggressive Ojibway hunter-warrior who would fight to the death.

Karl Menninger identifies anger as the common characteristic found in every individual who commits the act of suicide. In his book *Man Against Himself* (a title that aptly describes the dynamics at work within Chee Chee's life), Menninger theorizes that there are three components to the suicidal act, and that all are present in varying degrees in any given case: (1) the wish to kill, (2) the wish to be killed, and (3) the wish to die.[4] In the course of research on suicide notes, Edwin Shneidman and Norman Farberow asked Menninger to define those categories. Menninger responded, "I think you might use as a very rough criterion, conscious hate, conscious guilt feelings, and conscious hopelessness, or discouragement, as roughly determining the three components that I suggested."[5] These three components were precisely the feelings at work within Chee Chee when he killed himself. Menninger used additional descriptive terms to describe those three components: "wish to kill" – aggression, accusation, blame, eliminating, driving away, disposing of, annihilating, and revenge; "wish to be killed" – submission, masochism, self-blame, and self-accusation; "wish to die" – hopelessness, fear, fatigue, and despair.[6]

Aggressive feelings and clinical depression are closely connected. The emotional disorder identified as depression is difficult to define because it is not a single disorder with a single cause, but a multifaceted emotional problem. Theorists from the human sciences explain the problem of depression in ways ranging from inner personal dynamics to hormonal reactions. Most people at some point in their lives experience depression at one level or another, from the temporary experience of "the blues" to the more serious disorder of acute psychotic depression. Depression has been referred to as the common cold of psychopathology. It has been experienced throughout human history and has been recorded for centuries. It affects male and female, rich and poor, infant and elder. The authors of ancient theological classics noted the presence of accidie, or depression, in the lives of renowned spiritual leaders: "Put this sadness far from thee, for sadness is the sister of half-heartedness and bitterness" (Shepherd of Hermas); "Out of accidie comes despair" (St Gregory the Great); "The soul is cramped and hampered and imprisoned … Passive and sullen he withdraws into black sulkiness which can find no joy in God or men or the universe" (Dante Aligiere); "In accidie a man's stomach abhors all manner of meat" (St Thomas Acquinas); "It is a grief to him to live so that he himself hasteneth and desireth his own death" (Azanbite of Inwyt).[7]

Sigmund Freud understood anger as the underlying dynamic in depression, pointing out that devastating fury, which might have appropriately been turned against others, is turned against the self. If retroflexed rage is severe enough, it may lead to self-murder. Though all depressed persons do not become suicidal, and all individuals who kill themselves are not depressed, there is a substantial overlap between the experience of depression and the act of suicide. Depression possessed Chee Chee, and played an important role in his death.

John White, in his book *The Masks of Melancholy: A Christian Physician Looks at Depression and Suicide*, comments: "The distinguishing features of melancholia [a term Freud used for depression] are a profoundly painful dejection, abrogation of interest in the outside world, loss of the capacity to love, inhibition of all activity, and a lowering of the self-regarding feelings to a degree that finds utterance in self-reproaches and self-reviling, and culminates in a delusional expectation of punishment."[8] Freud connected depression to alienating experiences rooted in the formative years in the biological family. If a child lost a parent, or if parental love and support were withdrawn, Freud believed, the child would justifiably respond with feelings of rage and despair. Freud theorized that because of the difficulty of exteriorizing or venting anger towards the parent, the child would internalize the parent and make the parent a part of his own psyche. Then the child could safely express his rage and hostility. In the process the child turns the rage upon himself at an unconscious level, creating the symptoms of depression. This manner of responding to perceived rejection may become the way the individual deals with rejection generally and may continue to experience depressed feelings and behaviours throughout life.

Menninger's understanding of why people kill themselves is graphically depicted in his compelling catchphrase "man against himself." This phrase conveys the idea of a struggle to the death that goes on within the individual's inner life. Menninger believed that although we may not always fully comprehend what brought the person down, what is ultimately responsible is not to be found by examining the external forces on his or her life. To comprehend the motivations leading the individual to self-destruction, one must understand what is happening within the individual.

Describing the choice of suicide to deal with feelings of intolerable anguish, Menninger comments: "This method of dealing with life is determined either by some inherent constitutional variation, abnormality, or weakness in the individual or by the acceleration or powerful reinforcement of the destructive tendencies of the personality during the formative period of life. In either case it is apparent that the self-defeating tendencies arose very early in the life of the individual and strongly influenced the entire course of his development in such a way as to overshadow and finally conquer the benign life-instinct."[9] Menninger is of the opinion that individuals begin to commit suicide long before they in fact carry out the act. He identifies alcoholism and/or drug abuse as a chronic form of suicide: "The self-destructive consequences of alcoholism which are so obvious would seem to be, in part, incidental, that is, they are the untoward consequences of self-administered efforts at obtaining relief from internal dangers. As soon as these internal dangers threaten the destruction of the individual by his own impulses, alcoholism is chosen or substituted as a kind of lesser self-destruction serving to avert a greater self-destruction."[10] Hugh McKenzie told me that Chee Chee was heavily involved in the use of soft drugs and spent thousands of dollars on them.

The event that precipitated Chee Chee's final murderous attack upon himself was an occurrence that had happened to him many times. He got drunk, became offensive, and was arrested and thrown in jail following an altercation with the

police. The familiar scenario was usually played out by sober-
ing up, paying the fine, and leaving jail in the morning. But it
was not to be this time.

Frederick Brown's understanding of Chee Chee's death is
closely related to Menninger's concept of "man against himself." Brown says, "I think Benny revered himself as an artist
and hated himself as a person. He killed the person he hated,
and I think the reason he was fighting to live afterwards was
because he realized that he had killed the artist too. I think it
was a spur of the moment thing. It wasn't something that was
coming on by being mulled over and being decided. It was
not premeditated at all. It was an impulsive act occasioned by
the fact that the dreadful persona of Benjamin Chee Chee,
Indian drunk, had suddenly embarrassed and humiliated
Benjamin Chee Chee, the talented artist, to the point where
he couldn't stand it anymore … In the jail cell he had to get
rid of that terrible Indian drunk. That was the predominant
purpose of his action. Only afterwards did he subconscious-
ly realize he had also terminated the talented Indian artist,
and he fought for his life. The doctor told me he had never
seen anything like it as Benjamin fought to live."

8

HORIZONS OF HOPE: AN EMPOWERING JOURNEY

Our Brothers, Sisters, Friends
are dying one by one, with no warning

I don't know how to feel, how to act
Who will believe me
Who will understand
Who will listen

We couldn't stop them
The "only if" thoughts are forever spinning

I'm locked inside, I'm trapped
Inside I'm crying, screaming …
The hurt is bigger than me

Darkness, Mist, Fog
Unfocused, confused

Numbed, Silence, Floating
Shocking

Can't think beyond
Help us

Remove the lock
I'm tired

Let's open the door
I want to live and be free of hurt

Let's begin healing together
Begin the journey.

–Lillian Suganaqueb[1]

NISHNAWKE ASKI NATION YOUTH FORUM ON SUICIDE

The investigation of a suicide epidemic on the Wikwemikong Reserve on Manitoulin Island described in chapter 6 was conducted by psychiatrist John Ward, Native counsellor Joseph Fox, and myself, in the fall of 1976 and spring of 1977. This suicide epidemic involved a group of five males and three females, all single, in an age range from seventeen years to thirty-one years with a median age of twenty-two years. I was then an active member of the International Association of Suicide Prevention and Crisis Intervention, and we were to hold our biennial congress in Helsinki, in June 1977. I arranged to have my colleagues join me in the presentation of our study. As far as I am aware, it was the first occasion when the issue of Canadian aboriginal suicide was brought to the world's attention when our papers were published in the record of the congress.

Recently, a helpful critic suggested some material that would add significantly to this study, including a volume titled *Horizons of Hope: An Empowering Journey*, the work of the Nishnawbe Aski Nation Youth Forum on Suicide. That informative work has been useful in responding to questions of what is happening now with regard to issues regarding aboriginal suicide at the turn of the millennium. The information supports the substantial material on the issue taken from the 1996 *Report of the Royal Commission on Aboriginal Peoples.*

Nishnawbe Aski (NAN) is a place, and it is also a name of a people numbering approximately 28,000 men, women, and children. The community is comprised of forty-nine First Nation colonies located in Northern Ontario. Nishnawbe Aski connects Quebec in the east, Manitoba in the west, Hudson Bay and James Bay in the north and is bounded by the former Canadian National Rail ways in the south. It is a beautiful, rugged land of lakes and trees covering 200,000 square miles. The residents speak the Nishnawbe language that was commonly known as the Algonkian family language of Cree and Ojibway.

Most of the First Nations people in this remote area live in a land that is only accessible by air. For a brief period in winter some of those communities are also reachable through winter roads. Telephone service is generally available. Housing is inferior, lacking infrastructure such as water and sewer services. Adequate medical service is not available. As with most First Nation communities, there is little opportunity locally to gain an adequate education. Unemployment rates range up to 95 per cent. The available employment is seasonal.

What follows is a brief summary taken from the report generously supplied to me by those who created this insightful and particularly important work. The report describes the Nishnawbe-Aski culture as having been in a state of serious decline over the last four generations: "While some aspects of the culture are still readily apparent, much of the Aboriginal culture and spirituality have not been passed on in a systematic way. In some cases, it has been hidden or has not been clearly explained to the young people today."[2]

The authors explain that in Canadian society children are traditionally socialized through the training influences found in the home, family, and community, and all the variety of institutions and their rites of passage transmitting the culture's values. In Nishnawbe Aski, however, "these 'normal' means of socialization were systematically and deliberately undermined by the Canadian state and the church over the past 200 years. Beginning with residential schools, perhaps the harshest form of assimilation, attempts have been made to force Nishnawbe-Aski children to fit into mainstream society, to make them ashamed of who they are and to take away their language. Although residential schools no longer exist, the demoralizing impact of this abusive institution and the resulting cultural void continues to be felt by each successive generation. The present day generation of Youth are still victims of a system which sought to destroy Aboriginal culture and spirituality, which sought to destroy our connection to the land and to our language."[3]

The report describes how this assault on the Nishnawbe Aski culture by white society has produced several lost and confused generations, particularly with references to identity issues:

Many Nishnawbe-Aski young people are struggling with questions of who they are, and where they belong. They are exposed to a lavish lifestyle through the media, while attending urban high schools, and when travelling to larger centres; but the living conditions of their families and communities leave them with only the reality of extreme poverty. They are called "Indians", but they know that they are not "Indians". They know that their lifeline should be connected to the land and the resources, but nothing in the mainstream educational system or the media helps them build the connection. They wonder who they are or why they exist. Coupled with the physical, emotional and/or sexual abuse that has become intergenerational as a result of residential schools and loss of identity, it is not surprising that some young people decide it is easier to leave this world than continue to live in it. Suicide comes to be a viable alternative when there seems to be no hope to finding help or relief from an unending cycle of poverty and abuse: social, racial, physical and sexual.[4]

In a brief period of time the suicide rate began to reach startling levels, and it became clear the Nishnawbe Aski Nation was in the grip of a true suicide epidemic. From 1986 when four males and one female committed suicide, the death count grew to eighteen males and six females in 1995. By June 1996 there had been seven more completed suicides. In that brief period of ten years there had been more than 130 deaths! The majority of these suicides were committed by males between the ages of ten and twenty-five. Compared to Canadians in the same age group, the rate of suicide among the Nishnawbe-Aski Nation was three times greater.

Faced with the possibility that the future leaders of their culture, the brightest and the best, would be lost, the Nishnawbe Aski community and its leaders were driven to accept that they must somehow make a creative response to save their culture or lose everything that was precious to them. But first they needed to understand what was happening to them. What was it that had entered their world that could create such a hateful power and create such unspeakable destruction? They could sense its presence and the effect of its awesome power destroying of the lives of their young:

> The helplessness, pain and sadness is deep and runs throughout the community. People seem to be struggling as to how to begin the healing activities that must take place, especially for the peers of those who have died. The Youth are asking for someone who they can trust and turn to; someone to hear them and to help them according to their needs. The adults see and hear the pain of the Youth but are unsure about how to reach them. The adults want the Youth to listen to the teachings and take them in. The Youth, on the other hand, want the adults to acknowledge and understand their unique difficulties in growing up in today's world. They are looking for a way out of their confusion and sadness. They want relevant advice and guidance to help them cope positively with the stresses and losses that face them on a daily basis. Trust, support (instead of criticism) and teamwork appear to be the essential ingredients upon which to build a healing community. To begin the process of healing in the community, there needs to be strong leadership.[5]

But who would lead them in this investigation? That was the vital question. Generally that issue, particularly in aboriginal society, would have a foregone conclusion – the elders. But others, realizing the sorry state of their culture, had begun to consider otherwise. It was the young people who were being destroyed. Therefore it was they who must respond, if they were to be saved. A mixture of courage and a sense of desperation enabled the young people to grasp that truth. They were led by those like Lillian Suganaqueb, who wrote the stirring poem at the beginning of this chapter, desperately grasping at what appeared to be an impossible hope with those challenging words: "Let's begin healing together, / Begin the journey." The young people were being destroyed. They must save themselves. The report clearly indicates the direction they were to follow. Throughout the report they refer to themselves as "the Youth." It is a term that has a noble ring to it, young braves set to encounter an awesome foe.

This vision of being led by the young received strong support from the collective leadership of the Nishnawbe Aski Nation: "The inquiry would be headed by young people; the Youth would make the recommendations and Nishnawbe Aski Nation would ensure the recommendation were implemented. The idea was unique and foreign to some extent, as decisions are traditionally made by leaders and Elders. However, the concept received strong support by the collective leadership and Nishnawbe Aski Nation and the Nishnawbe Aski Nation Youth Forum on Suicide was established."[6]

A rescue mission of this nature is not formed overnight, nor will the hoped-for results be immediate. Its goals needed to be carefully established. Its central mission must be one that leads from a direction of self-destruction towards the goal of growth and development. The process would require the total involvement of all concerned. Though the suicide forum would be led by the youth, the wisdom of the old was recognized and viewed as a necessity. The presence and the wisdom of men such as Chief Ignace Gull was required, and sought, his words weighed carefully: "If the world is to be brought to order, my Nation must be changed. If my Nation is to be changed, my community reserve must be made over. If my reserve is to be reordered, my family must be set right. If my family is to be regenerated, I myself must be first."[7]

The intent of the forum was to bring the issue of self-destruction into the open. Why were people killing themselves? Why was it the youth who were the victims? It was hoped that this process would lead to answers to those awful questions. Then, how could healing responses be followed? How could different lifestyles be introduced that would eventually halt the deepening disaster driving a people to destroy themselves?

In the beginning the skill of communication had to be learned, particularly the ability to express at the feeling level: "When a loved one passes away, you are told to be strong and not cry. This is the old fashioned way. We need to cry it out soon, then we will feel better afterwards. If one doesn't cry, the pain and hurt will forever stay there. In order to heal ourselves, we have to face the truth and reality and not hide away anymore."[8]

To become more open, the ability to trust needed to be established. The report noted: "Some adults see that Youth have difficulty expressing their feelings; to talk about what is bothering them emotionally, as well as what is bothering them mentally. This inability to express feelings is directly related to the lack of and inability to trust. The trust issue is the most essential ingredient of the helping relationship. Trust must exist if people are going to share, talk about their hurt and pain and find ways to empower themselves to heal. The lack of trust and the subsequent inability to speak privately and openly is cited as the main reason for the significant amount of substance and solvent abuse."[9]

The report connects the issue of depression and suicide

deaths and lack of trust to attitudes learned in childhood experiences: "Adults see the relationship between the onset of depression and suicide deaths and attempts. The suicide problem finds its roots in traumatic events such as family violence, sexual and/or physical abuse, substance abuse, death of friends due to suicide, the grinding pain of the grieving process, and previous thoughts and/or attempts at suicide. These traumatic events lead to negative thinking and to suicidal thinking. This coupled with a host of unhealthy, self-defeating behaviours (such as drinking, sniffing, drugging) are used to cope with the underlying trauma. This in turn, leads to layers of hurt, affecting the individual concerned and potential generations of unresolved issues and negative coping mechanisms."[10]

Suicide may be viewed as a method of communication by those who lack the ability to communicate otherwise. Under the heading "Suicide Is a Cry for Help" is an attempt to describe what lies in the back of the mind of the suicidee: "The people that commit suicide, it is a cry for help. They are saying there is something wrong here – help me. Some may say things like I am going to kill myself, or I am going to shoot myself. They give out signs and if we don't hear the signs, then it does become a successful suicide. They have succeeded in what they wanted to do, but if we could have prevention and intervention before these things actually take place, it would benefit a lot of our people."[11]

One young Native describes the process of developing wrong thinking that eventually arrives at extremely dangerous conclusions: "When I was about eight years old, that is when I started gas sniffing. When I experienced the loss of my aunt's children that died in the fire, that is when I started to think about what I was doing to myself. I was abusing solvents, gas, and doing drugs at the same time. When I was doing the sol-vent gas sniffing in the bush by myself, a lot of times I would think about what is the use of going on living. I would even experiment trying to hang myself in the bush. The more I got into the gas sniffing, the more that thought about wanting to commit suicide and doing away with myself – thinking of what is the use of going on to live. Also, watching my parents drink the way they did, I started to think I was to blame for their drinking."[12]

The sharing of these feelings and personal experiments brought others to understand that they were caught up in the same process, going through the same pain. It enabled them to develop a closeness to begin to work together to combat their common problem:

When suicide hits this community, everybody gets help-less, wondrous and hopeless. Great pains, aches, starts to appear once again. People start to do things, such as cut-ting their wrists with sharp knives, razor blades, glass or anything that is very sharp. Many of the teenagers that I know, including myself, are doing sniffing, drinking, smoking hash and bringing narcotics into this communi-ty. I don't know who will stop this situation, not even the police or community leaders. This community needs a lot of help from outside and inside … Sometimes I'm feeling that I'll do the same thing just like friends did. These easy thoughts come up early into my head … Our Elders encourage us a lot not to commit suicide, but still inside me, there's suicide. We even try to help each other in recreation, but most of the teens aren't there. That's where the hurt began to reappear. Thinking about there should have been a lot more teens, and flashbacks – this really hurts if you're an athlete, knowing the right person is not there anymore. I hope government officials recognize what I've been trying to say.[13]

Working through this report, experiencing the feelings of these people, one cannot help but be caught up in the agony of a culture struggling to turn back a terrible force destroying their young people. They are fully aware that they alone can save themselves. Much as one would want to effect a rescue operation, that change must come from within.

The report identifies negative factors that contribute to self-destructive behaviour:

Attending boarding/residential school
All kinds of judging and blaming
The feeling of being judged, especially by the dominant society
Blaming others and engaging in negative gossip
Blaming self: giving yourself constant negative messages, like "I'm ugly"; "It's my fault"
Judging others and being judgmental: essentially engaging in behaviours that hurt others
The feeling of not belonging;
The feeling of deep loneliness
Feeling hurt, shame and guilt;
Feeling numb: like you have no feelings
Feeling personal pain;
Feeling a lack of support and encouragement for your life and your dreams
Unemployment
The experience of growing up with alcoholic parents and being part of a dysfunctional family

Violence in the presence of children, i.e. to witness
    physical abuse and fighting between parents and child
The peer pressure of friends especially around behaviours
    of smoking-up and drinking
Violent and abusive interpersonal relationships
Vicious, brutal beatings of a sexual or physical nature
Being fatherless insofar as the father is not present, or
    if present, is acutely, emotionally disinterested and
    unattached to the family structure
Alcohol abuse
Jail.[14]

Of the negative factors mentioned, the most common
among the adult presentations were alcohol abuse, sexual
abuse, violence in the presence of children, and blaming.

Positive factors identified as being important and vital to a
more healthy life were also included in the presentations:

Sobriety
The belief that we all have a purpose
Loving each other
Belief in a life that includes the Creator/Great Spirit
Prayer
Traditional teachings
Respect for all of life
Pride in ourselves and positive self-esteem
Education
Culture
Native Language
A place for our Elders and the wisdom to follow
    their teachings
Accepting ourselves as the Creator has made us
Accepting our gifts as given to us by the Creator

The sense of ownership
Strong and positive role models
Native treatment programs in our community
Support groups in our community.[15]

One young Native expressed a new life experience we hope all would one day know: "Since I have sobered up, I have accomplished many things. Today, my sober life has been good to me. I have taken back all the old teachings from my grandmothers' traditions and culture that we have, we Native people … this is an eagle feather I found a couple of weeks before I stopped drinking. I always wanted an eagle feather and I found this on the road. I've been sober ever since. I was told by my grandmothers, 'respect these birds.' That's all creation. The Creator made these … It was like my prayers were answered and I am proud of the eagle feather today. I am proud of all the animals and birds and all the people today. I respect people. Creator gives us life. Today I meditate in mornings, meditate in evening."[16]

A hopeful note appears at the end of the report:

One thing that is very important to understand is that healing usually begins from within individuals that make up the community. There are a lot of communities well on their way to healing. I see it as a very positive step for our Nations, that is beginning to look at the issues that have, for so long, prevented us from being able to live our life comfortably the way we were meant to. To me, there is hope for our culture, for our identities, and hope for our futures. When people come up and talk about their painful issues and painful memories, I have great admiration for them because it is a very courageous step toward building healthy communities and a brighter future for our children. The more we get together as people and begin to look at our pain together, the stronger we become as people, as Nations. In closing, I would like to encourage all the people to continue on the path of healing and the path of recovery. I am sure once the message gets out for the rest of our people, we will be able to assert ourselves as the people of what our Creator intended us to be ... that is proud, healthy Aboriginal people.[17]

The Nishnawbe Aski Nation Youth Forum on Suicide was created near the end of the twentieth century. It expresses the hope that this healing process will occur throughout the First Nation culture and lead to a significant change in the self-destructive behaviour that has marked the lives of young Canadian Natives for so many years. Generations will likely pass before the anticipated changes develop. Nevertheless, the determination of these young Natives to create positive change is promising. We join with them in their aspiration: "May the Creator continue to give us strength in our journeys."[18]

9

THE HEALING

Everything can be taken away from a man but one thing –
the last of the human freedoms – to choose one's attitude in
any circumstance, to choose one's own way.

–Viktor Frankl

In 1989 the oil carrier *Exxon Valdez*, loaded to capacity, went
aground on the rocky coast of Alaska. What followed was
reported to be one of the most horrendous oil spills in mar-
itime history. The site of the accident created worldwide concern as some forty thousand tons of oily sludge washed up on
the pristine shores of Alaska. It was a terrible disaster. We were
convinced that the natural beauty of a remote wilderness
environment would be ruined forever, despite the frantic
efforts that were immediately initiated.

Recently some fresh information about the accident surprised me and gave me much-needed reassurance that while
an environmental disaster can occur, apparently beyond
repair, there remains the creative powers of nature to put
things right again. Hope came as I listened to Bob Clarke, a
marine biologist and consultant on pollution from Aberdeen
University in Scotland, speaking on the World Service of the
BBC. He was responding to the report of a large oil spill that
had happened that very day, 2 July 1997. This time another oil

carrier, the *Diamond Grace*, had scraped its hull against a reef in Tokyo Bay, releasing some 13,400 tons of crude oil. A massive oil slick was now threatening the coast of Japan. Some seventy ships were at the scene, their crews pouring chemicals into the sea in an effort to minimize the damage.

Clarke stated, with convincing confidence, that whatever the damage, nature would clean up the mess in relatively short order. His time frame was "a couple of years." He was quite certain that the environment would be restored to its previous condition. Though I received Clarke's optimistic statement with scepticism, I later learned that he spoke with such authority because of his experience. He had been present at the *Exxon Valdez* cleanup for the first three years. He had recently returned to the scene of the accident on the Alaska coast and had toured areas that had been subject to cleanup efforts by an army of volunteers as well as areas where the cleanup had been left to nature. Both areas had been restored to their former state of beauty! He claimed that the restorative power of nature would eventually restore any damage done to the coast of Japan just as it had erased the damage done by the *Exxon Valdez*.

There is ample evidence of a restorative healing force within nature. From the gravity of serious physical wounds to the profound damage to hundreds of thousands of trees by forest fires, it is evident that nature's drive to survive, to heal, and to live is not easily thwarted. Despite a fire in 1988 that apparently destroyed over a million hectares of forest, the beauty of Yellowstone Park is now being restored. The science of medicine supports the healing forces already at work within the body to obliterate disease and restore the organism to health and well-being.

Is it possible that the healing of a nation as deeply wounded as that of Canadian Natives can take place? Recently I sat with a group of Natives and non-Natives to listen to the strengthening rhythm of the ceremonial drum and the uplifting message the Native speaker brought to us. We were made aware of the terrible damage inflicted upon Native people and its effects that had been passed from generation to generation. Against this revelation of hurt was the steady pulsing of the great drum, like a strong healthy heartbeat, a healing power that would not be denied. I felt a surge of optimism.

"Ceremonial drums are constructed in a ritual manner. Their sound is described as the heartbeat of the nation or the heartbeat of the universe," notes the 1996 Royal Commission report. The Dene nation describes the ceremonial drum as an important symbol of unity: "The drum represents unity of self, others, the spiritual world, and land."[1] Long after the meeting I could still hear the drum beat. I continued to hear the words of the Native speaker. His message was that a healing was taking place in the lives of First Nation people, and this developing sense of well-being was related to the rediscovery of their spiritual roots.

Healing is like a young plant struggling for life in a barren land. It needs nurturing. But who can offer the nourishment to sustain the growth? What can restore health? I continue to be aware of the words of a Native woman as she spoke about the residential school system, an experience that had scarred her for life. She said: "This was our holocaust. They did not kill us physically, but they killed us emotionally and spiritually."[2]

She had selected the correct and penetrating term: what has happened, and is happening to the Native people of Canada, is a holocaust. The process, once begun, has continued for generations. Those who were abused have become abusers. Problems within the Native community are compounded by white society which views the Native people as a problem that will not go away. Attitudes of rejection once held by members of white society have generally been replaced by expressions of confusion, uncertainty, and irritability. Recognition, approval, and respect for Native people is still withheld.

Assimilation may be characterized as a form of genocide. The process began long ago. The words of Duncan Campbell Scott, deputy superintendent-general of Indian Affairs, in a speech given in 1920 before a parliamentary committee, clearly state that the intent was to erase the Native culture: "Our objective is to continue until there is not a single Indian in Canada that has not been absorbed into the body politic and there is no Indian question, and no Indian Department."[3] The aboriginal people were to be erased. It was a holocaust.

Holocaust is an aggressive term. If there is any doubt about the aggressive intent of the federal government, one need only turn to the section of the Royal Commission report that deals with residential schools to note the violent terms used in connection with the clear goal of the program:

At the heart of the vision of residential education – a vision of the school as home and sanctuary of motherly care – there was a dark contradiction, an inherent element of savagery in the mechanics of civilizing the children. The very language in which the vision was couched revealed what would have to be the essentially violent nature of the school system in its assault on child and culture. The basic premise of re-socialization, of the great transformation from "savage" to "civilized," was violent. "To kill the Indian in the child", the department aimed at severing the artery of culture that ran between generations and was the profound connection between parent and child sustaining family and community. In the end, at the point of final assimilation, "all the Indian there is in the race should be dead." This was more than a rhetorical flourish as it took on a traumatic reality in the life of each child separated from parents and community and isolated in a world hostile to identity, traditional belief and language.[4]

White culture was a force that was to destroy and deeply wound countless Natives. Many became suicidal and turned upon themselves. Others turned their anger upon families and communities. The psychologist Abraham Maslow is clear about the source of negative forces within human nature. He was firmly of the opinion that humans are not inherently evil. He taught that people have an inborn nature that is essentially good or neutral. As they mature, their creative aspects naturally manifest themselves more clearly. Then what is it that undermines and destroys human beings so filled with potential and promise?

Maslow's insights into the complexities of human nature came at a critical time, turning the science of psychology in new and fresh directions. He established that humans become miserable or neurotic because the environment has made them so through ignorance and social pathology. Maslow was emphatic that destructiveness is not inherent in human nature, but that human beings are twisted by external forces beyond their control that change and destroy their humanness.[5]

If we have any doubt about the source of the self-destruction within aboriginal people, we have only to ask one question: "How many young Natives have experienced a similar destiny to that of Benjamin Chee Chee?" Their numbers are legion. Among the Native people of Canada there are many young, promising men and women who yet harbour an inner self-destructive urge. They have been conditioned to feel unsure of themselves, confused about who they are, where they belong, and who they want to be as they try to work out a life for themselves within white culture.

Most Canadians believe they are not personally involved in the damage inflicted upon the Native people, though they would admit that they have not fared well in our culture. As the Royal Commission report notes, "The vast majority of non-Aboriginal Canadians who have given any thought to the matter would probably acknowledge that Canada's Aboriginal peoples have not been accorded their proper place in the life and constitution of this country. Some might say that this is attributable to deep-seated racism, others might say, more charitably, that it is the result of the paternalistic, colonial attitude we have described, the goal of which was to indoctrinate the original inhabitants of Canada into the ways of non-Aboriginal society and make them over in the image of the newcomers."[6]

Since our culture is the source of the problem, and we are part of that culture, many Canadians would like to reverse the process but do not know how to begin. No doubt some white people have been helpful to Native people. As Chief John Beaver of the Alderville Indian Reserve on Rice Lake once said in an interview, "Those people in Ottawa are not ogres!" Of course not. But too often, despite their best intentions, they have been insensitive and ill-informed. Generally the nature of the help offered, unknowingly based on white arrogance, has been ruinous.

Subtle conditioning has infected members of the white race with a sense of superiority over all others. This sense of superiority has generally not penetrated personal awareness. These feelings are masked and manifested in terms of paternalism and condescension. This kind of attitude is racist, and it is always poisonous. To ensure that the help we are offering will be truly helpful, we need to scrutinize continually our own motives for wanting to help and search out the hidden agendas. Most important is the need to evaluate fully the effect our help is having on the helpee.

The word "help" itself creates difficulties. It implies taking care of, rescuing, protecting. Help of that nature is not growth oriented and leads people in the opposite direction from personal development. The help that we have offered to Native people continues to be paternalistic. The dynamics of paternalism are almost impossible to break because the subjects become more and more dependent, eventually losing all ability to break free and initiate change. The only type of help that offers the possibility of authentic growth and change is the help we give ourselves.

This understanding enabled Viktor Frankl to survive the holocaust in which he was caught. Frankl was born in Vienna. He was Jewish, a psychiatrist by profession. Early during World War II he was arrested and thrown into a concentration camp. Miraculously he survived. He credits a form of psychotherapy which he began to develop in the concentration camp for saving his life. It is called Logotherapy, a self-help therapy related to the need for the experience of meaningfulness. In the concentration camp Frankl experienced the loss of everything he had ever loved and wanted. He lost family, colleagues, and friends. He lost his vocation, status in society, wealth, home, and belongings. He lost the freedom to go where he wanted. He lost his freedom of speech.

One thing remained. Frankl writes, "We who lived in con-centration camps can remember the men who walked through the huts comforting others, giving away their last piece of bread. They may have been few in number but they offered sufficient proof that everything can be taken away from a man but one thing: the last of the human freedoms - to choose one's attitude in any circumstance, to choose one's way."[7] Frankl was stripped to the bone of everything but his own personal attitude to life and living. All around him were death and destruction. People were dying in the furnaces, by their own hand, or of despair. The equation of despair is hopelessness plus helplessness: "There is no hope and there is nothing further I can do." Frankl did not agree. He believed that no one but himself could control his attitudinal response to the circumstances of life.

The German theologian Paul Tillich has pointed out that certain kinds of anxieties – situational anxiety, separation anx-iety, and free-floating or chronic anxiety – can be treated suc-cessfully, but existential anxiety cannot. Yet it is a useful anxi-ety. It is one of the main sources that spurs us to keep on liv-ing and searching to discover the fullness of life. Existential anxiety is related to issues of meaning, purpose, and direction. It constantly disturbs us with questions like: "Who am I?" "What is life?" "Where do I fit into the rhythm of life?" "Why was I created?" "Where do I find a meaningful existence?"

Chief Jacob Thomas, a hereditary chief of the Cayuga Nation and a ceremonialist among the Six Nations of the Iroquois in both Canada and the United States, refers to the existential issues raised in the Native experience: "Since the time of Creation the population of the Onkwehonweh were instructed. That's why we always go back to the time of

Creation. We were always instructed from that time: Where
did we come from? And what's our purpose in being here?
And how did that tradition come about?"[8] As a deeply spiritual people, aboriginals had answers to those questions. They
knew who they were. They knew about the why of creation.
They knew where they fit into the great plan of creation. The
knew they were part of the creativity of the Great Spirit. They
knew to whom they were responsible. In the *Report of the
Royal Commission on Aboriginal Peoples* we read:

> The fundamental feature of Aboriginal world view was,
> and continues to be, that all of life is a manifestation of
> spiritual reality. We come from spirit, we live and move
> surrounded by spirit; and when we leave this life we
> return to a spirit world. All perceptions are conditioned
> by spiritual forces, and all actions have repercussions in
> a spiritual reality. Actions initiated in a spiritual realm
> affect physical reality, conversely, human actions set off
> consequences in a spiritual realm. These consequences
> in turn become manifest in the physical realm. All these
> interactions must be taken into account as surely as con-
> siderations of what to eat or how to keep warm in win-
> ter ... Exploration of Aboriginal belief systems demon-
> strates that for diverse peoples, their world was filled
> with mystery, but there were rules and personal guides,
> in the form of wisdom handed down from ancestors and
> spirit helpers who were available, if properly
> approached, to aid them in pursuit of a good life. It was
> the responsibility of every person to learn the rules, to
> acquire the measure of spiritual power appropriate to
> his or her situation, and to exercise that power in accor-
> dance with the ethical system given to the whole society

as "wisdom." Failure to do so would have repercussions not only for the individual; his or her transgressions of spiritual law could cause hardship for family members and associates in the community.[9]

The word *spiritual* has the same root as *spire* (the summit of something or to point upward), *spiral* (advancing, increasing, and continually developing), and to *aspire* (to long for and to desire). Spirituality has always been an essential part of the aboriginal life experience. For many Natives this is a perspective that has been lost, and if the healing is to continue, must be rediscovered. A Native elder told the commissioners, "When I hear people say: 'We've lost this; we've lost that', I do not believe that. We have not lost anything, we have just forgotten ... we are coming out of a big sleep ... We are waking up, and it's a beautiful thing, to wake up and see we are alive, we are still here."[10] The words bring to mind those of T.S. Eliot at the end of his *Four Quartets*:

We shall not cease from exploration
And the end of all our exploring
Will be to arrive where we started,
And know the place for the first time.

Faced with the holocaust of Hitler's Third Reich, Frankl reflected on his own existence. He viewed the search for meaning as being of the greatest significance. As a consequence, he developed this profound wisdom: "Again and again we have seen that an appeal to continue life, to survive the most unconditional conditions, can be made only when such survival appears to have meaning. That meaning must be specific and personal, a meaning which can be realized by that person alone. For we must never forget that every man is unique in the universe. I remember my dilemma in a concentration camp when faced with a man and a woman who were close to suicide; both had told me that they had expected nothing more in life. I asked both my fellow prisoners whether the question was really what we expected from life. Was it not, what life was expecting from us. I suggested that life was awaiting something from them. In fact the woman was being awaited by her child abroad, and the man had a series of books which he had begun to write and publish but had not finished."[11]

Reading Frankl's words, I came finally to the truth he was trying to teach me. Frankl did not have in mind the process of *contemplating* meaning. He was urging us to *do* meaning. To find meaning in life requires that we do meaningful things and act in meaningful ways. His book *The Doctor and the Soul* offers further clarification: "But if the patient should object that he does not know the meaning of his life, that the unique potentialities of his existence are not apparent to him, then we can only reply that his primary task is just this: to find his way to his own proper task, to advance toward the uniqueness and singularity of his own meaning in life. As for this matter of each man's inner potentialities – in other words, how a man is to go about learning what he ought to be from what he is – there is no better answer than that given by Goethe: 'How can we learn to know ourselves? Never by reflection, but by action. Try to do your duty and you will soon find out what you are. But what is your duty? The demands of each day.'"[12]

Frankl suggests three elements which when present indicate that life is being lived meaningfully: creating something or doing a worthwhile act; opening yourself to new experience or a new relationship; developing a viable attitude to unavoidable suffering. How we live and respond to life is ultimately our own responsibility. We cannot be dragged kicking and screaming into a meaningful life. It must be an independent action. Ultimately our life journey is our personal response to creation. In the end we are responsible for our own growth and development, for whether we will live or die. The final choice lies in the attitudes we develop towards our life circumstances. One of Frankl's most important revelations is that meaningfulness is a healing force. He wrote: "The spiritual dimension cannot be ignored, for it is what makes us human."[13] By connecting with and endeavouring to satisfy the existential need of meaning, we also give our lives a sense of purpose and direction. In doing so we open ourselves to the strengthening, cleansing, restorative resources of nature. We develop a living connection with the world of the numinous – the domain of the spirit. We are put in touch with the resources that will enable us to become fully human. Despite the losses aboriginal people have endured, no one can take away "the last of the human freedoms – to choose one's attitude in any circumstance." Their healing lies in an experience that has always been with them – the presence of the Great Spirit. The rediscovery of Native spirituality and the development of a creative attitude will ensure that the healing now begun continues.

The commissioners confirm this: "In our report on suicide among Aboriginal people, Choosing Life, we wrote of the role played by culture stress and the erosion of ethical values in the genesis of suicidal behaviour. Merle Beedie, an elder who lived through successive placements in four residential schools, confirmed from her own experience that reclaiming traditions was a source of self-confidence and self-esteem: 'When I talk about the changing attitudes of some – the evidence is already happening in our communities, changing the attitudes about what we want to do just by us following the Anishnabe [Ojibway] road. Some of us are beginning to realize what good people we are. I'm becoming a better person because I'm following some of our traditional values. As we learn more and more of these things we become stronger and stronger.'[14]

The rediscovery of their spiritual heritage is neither a magic formula nor a sign that the struggle by Native people to regain their health and well-being has ended. But it is the path that they are to follow, a place on which to stand. It is the source from which they will derive wisdom and other creative resources, the assurance that the promise of freedom to be who they were created to be will be fulfilled. The sinews holding their community together, now torn and shredded, will be restored only if Native people follow the direction in which the spiritual path leads them. The resources they need will then be revealed by the Great Spirit alive once more in them.

Canadians generally are troubled about the predicament of Native people. They are informed daily through the media of traumatic events occurring in Native communities and wonder what they can do. A number of years ago I was contacted by a young woman, newly graduated from a school of social work, who had been appointed as a counsellor to Native people living on a reserve in Northern Saskatchewan. She asked if I could give her some advice on how best to help. I responded immediately: "Don't go!" Naturally she was very disappointed with my response. But over the years I have seldom met a professional caregiver from white society who has successfully and usefully related to members of the Native community. The block is usually the impossibility of establishing a basis of trust. The "fundamental work of unlocking the wellsprings of health within themselves"[15] belongs to Native people themselves. White society's function is to open the way – "to remove the obstacles." No easy task, for the way is blocked by an almost impenetrable jungle of political and legal undergrowth. Native leaders and their consultants, and government officials and their advisors, are struggling to clear a passage – with some success. Those of us who stand by must remain alert to what is happening, applaud the progress as the passage toward self-determination is opened, and not get in the way.

The *Report of the Royal Commission on Aboriginal Peoples* is a treasure trove for those who seek to know and understand Native people. Deep in the centre of this massive study is a brief statement that gives clear direction to all those who have been involved in the suffocating morass of the past. Though this section deals specifically with the family, and the statement appropriately comes under "Community Healing and Structural Change," the essence of the recommendation may be viewed as all-encompassing:

> The elements of the strategy include changing the political and economic conditions that now have negative effects on Aboriginal nations, communities, families and individuals, restructuring service delivery through healing centres and lodges under Aboriginal control; adopting measures to develop Aboriginal human resources to

support community planning and self-care; and making
the social institutional environment of Canadian society
more hospitable to Aboriginal cultures and identities. The
fundamental work of unlocking the wellsprings of health
within themselves belongs to Aboriginal people. The role
of Canadian governments and public policy is to remove
the obstacles under their control and ensure that
resources to support whole health are distributed equi-
tably between Aboriginal nations and communities and
the rest of Canadian society.[15]

10

FINAL WORDS

Bright as the arc of the air
My brush claims a bird
In his flight
Sun silvered, his wings
Sweep my canvas
In flight
                    –Daphne McLaughlin

Following an elaborate funeral service in the Native tradition, Benjamin Chee Chee's body was buried at the Notre Dame Cemetery in Ottawa on 18 March 1977. In February 1997, Ron Corbett, a reporter for the *Ottawa Sun*, was assigned to write a story to commemorate the twentieth anniversary of Chee Chee's death. In the process of researching his assignment Corbett discovered that Chee Chee's grave had remained unmarked for those twenty years except for a beaded stick placed there by a ten-year-old Native child.

Corbett's story is headlined "Unmarked grave almost all that's left of one of Ottawa's most prolific artists." This headline is followed by another in large, bold type: "PILLAGED LEGACY." The story begins with Corbett's experience with the receptionist at the cemetery:

The woman walks to a steel filing cabinet and asks how you spell the last name. "Chee Chee," I reply, "C-H-E-E, c-h-e-e, first name Benjamin." She nods her head and pulls open a drawer, starts flipping through index cards. It is raining outside, the ground covered with a light fog. Through the window of the office I can see ice forming on the 20 foot, eight-women-carrying-a-sculpted-coffin tomb of Sir Wilfrid Laurier. 'Are you a family member?' 'No, I'm a reporter: I'm working on a story.' She nods her head again, but doesn't show any interest. She keeps flipping the index cards. "I thought the name sounded familiar: Chee Chee. People come in every once in awhile and ask about him. Yes, here it is." She pulls out an index card and looks at it. "He is in Section 63." She walks to the counter and places the card in front of me. I start reading: Benjamin Chee Chee, buried in Grave 828, Section 63, his plot paid for twenty years ago this month by the Ottawa Friendship Centre. There is a woman's name for next of kin, but no address. There is nothing else. "That's an unmarked grave," the woman says, taking the card back. "It's strange to have an unmarked grave in that section. People come in, every few years, and talk to us about putting a marker on it. Nothing ever comes of it though." "Do you know who he was," I ask? The woman moves her shoulders slightly, closes the drawer of the filing cabinet as quietly as possible. "I don't know for sure, but I'm told he used to be famous. Some sort of artist." I nod my head and walk outside.[1]

The tone of Corbett's article is angry, aimed particularly at those who had seized the opportunity to use Chee Chee's death to make money. He reports a comment by Guy Mattar, the lawyer who has handled the Chee Chee estate through the years: "The list of people who did well is a long one. Maybe the only person in Ottawa who never profited from Benjamin Chee Chee was Benjamin Chee Chee."[2] Corbett raises questions of illegality and unethical behaviour: "What happened to Chee Chee's art after his death – to his money and his estate – is a story arguably as tragic as the life that preceded it, a tale rife with intrigue, claims and counter-claims, RCMP investigations and a lot of people who, at the end of the day, despite all the furor, profited handsomely."[3]

Corbett notes that Chee Chee had two wishes. The first of these was to create an art form that needed no signature. The second was to be known, to be remembered, and treated with respect:

Strange that one wish came to be so utterly fulfilled, the other so utterly betrayed. When I find Chee Chee's grave on that rainy, February day, marked anonymously with a wooden cross and beads that someone has placed in his honor, I can't help but think about that. A man such as Chee Chee, so vibrant and full of life, a man who painted images that have travelled the world, like his birds, buried in a grave that does not even mention his name. One of the greatest artists Canada has ever produced, certainly one of the most colorful and innovative, a man who made money for countless people during his life and in the two decades that followed it, yet no one has seen fit to grant his second wish. To be remembered. To have people say, "Look, there's Benjamin Chee Chee." No one. What passes for shame in this day and age? For a long time after leaving Notre Dame Cemetery, I wonder about that.[4]

When the media broke the news, the immediate response was a tombstone on Grave 828, Section 63, with Chee Chee's countenance and a reproduction of one of his famous paintings of wild geese etched on the polished black granite. Guilt can be a powerful motivator. Chee Chee had become an embarrassment, and it was necessary to rebury him. The ceremony was done with the appropriate speeches and prayers. The mayors of Vanier and Ottawa declared a Benjamin Chee Chee Day. Asked for her comment, his mother, Josephine Roy, who was present to unveil the tombstone, quietly responded: "Thank you very much."[5] It would have been interesting to know what was going on in her mind.

The long-unmarked grave was neither an intended rebuff nor an accidental oversight. It was symbolically consistent with Chee Chee's enigmatic life. He always yearned for acceptance and respect. Though it was offered to him on many occasions, he could not accept it. He was blocked by a major handicap in his personality – the inability to receive love and approval. Being orphaned early, living a third of his life in penal institutions, addicted to alcohol and drugs, trapped in the tentacles of the existence of a Canadian Native, prepared him for a place in an unmarked pauper's grave.

I wonder if he is restless under the burden of that massive, expensive tombstone. I think he would have been more comfortable lying with his forefathers in the simplicity and beauty of the graveyard at Bear Island on Lake Temagimi. That was the wisdom of the National Indian Brotherhood. They knew where he belonged, and they had wanted his body buried at Bear Island. Josephine was understandably concerned about carrying her son's body across the fragile ice of Lake Temagimi in early spring. She had lost his father under those same conditions. Benjamin was buried in the city.

Though he was unable to accept love, there were many who did love him. For a number of years friends and associates attempted valiantly to raise funds to purchase the headstone. These included Ernie Bies and the Ottawa Native Concerns

Committee, a group of aboriginal and non-aboriginal persons working together to advance First Nations issues. A number of fund-raising projects were started shortly after his death but to no avail. In early 1997 it was decided to involve the media to gain publicity for a fund-raising campaign. Hundreds came forward with contributions. "When I discovered that he was buried in an unmarked grave, I just couldn't believe it," said Alex Akiwenzie, president of the Ottawa Native Concerns Committee. "Everyone in the native community knows who Benjamin Chee Chee was."[6] In a fund-raising letter Akiwenzie wrote: "At issue is First Nations artist Benjamin Chee Chee who died almost 20 years ago in Ottawa. In death, Benjamin was freed from an existence of addiction and confusion. He suffered abuses at the Alfred Training School for boys, yet somehow, was one of the first Native painters, who with the fine lines and colour of Aboriginal style, captured the appreciation of art connoisseurs the world over. But Benjamin Chee Chee who did not live to realize his full potential continues in death to be treated unfairly."[7]

In an article published in *Windspeaker*, the Native journal, Murray Angus comments: "According to Akiwenzie, there was no clear reason why Chee Chee's grave went unmarked for so long. He said, 'It seems that, at the time, everybody thought someone else was going to do something. But in the end, nobody did.'"[8]

Truly people did love Chee Chee, and he was revered among his own people. But it was difficult to engage with him. He tended to thwart the best of intentions. Ironically, even in death the same frustrating processes continued to be at work. Nevertheless, his art, the expression of his genius and real humanness, touched people deeply, and continues to do so, guiding them into a deeper, richer inner life's experience. These spiritual feelings were felt by Daphne McLaughlin after first seeing Chee Chee's paintings. That experience inspired her to write a poem which she sent to him. He loved the poem, pleased that someone had recognized that part of his personality. The poem was used in the eulogy at his funeral service in 1977:

Bright as the arc of the air
My brush claims a bird
In his flight
Sun silvered, his wings
Sweep my canvas
In light.

My paint swims in rainbows
The fish flash,
Flowing where their waters run:
The curve of my brush
Flows silver by rock
And by stone.

My brush in my land
Of the White Pine,
Makes legend the moose
And the bear.
Mighty, the lords of the forest
Stand there.

–Daphne McLaughlin

NOTES

CHAPTER TWO

1 E. Bies, "The End of the Wild Ride."

2 William Blake, "The Little Boy Lost."

3 G. Watson, "Portrait of an Artist."

4 E. Bies, "End of the Wild Ride."

5 Ibid., 7.

6 Ibid., 18.

7 "A Great Artist," letter to the editor, *Ottawa Citizen*, 31 March 1977.

8 Nancy Baele, "Chee Chee's Work Needs No Signature."

9 G. Watson, "Portrait of an Artist."

10 Rudy Platiel, *Toronto Globe and Mail*, circa 15 March 1977.

11 Rudy Platiel, "Success of Ojibwa Painter Underlines Haunting Legacy."

CHAPTER THREE

1 William Fleming, *Art, Music and Ideas*.

2 In J. Clark and R. Houle, eds., *Benjamin Chee Chee*.

3 *Ottawa Journal*, 31 August 1974.

4 Ibid.

5 E. Bies, *Arts West*.

6 Traditional Ojibway Funeral Planned for Indian Artist, *Toronto Globe and Mail*, circa 13 March 1977.

7 Elizabeth McLuhan, *Painting and Prints in the Collection of the Thunder Bay National Exhibition Centre and Centre for Indian Art*.

8 Ibid.

9 Ibid.

10 Ernie Bies, correspondence with Norm Socha, 1 February 1979.

11 Quoted in Clarke/Irwin publications calendar, 1977.

12 Nancy Baele, "Chee Chee's Work Needs No Signature."

13 Ibid.

14 In J. Clark and R. Houle, eds., *Benjamin Chee Chee.*

15 Ibid.

16 Ibid.

17 Ibid.

18 Arthur Creighton, *The Life and Death of Benjamin Chee Chee.*

19 Wayne Edmonstone, "The Dying of Chee Chee."

20 Ibid.

21 In J. Clark and R. Houle, eds., *Benjamin Chee Chee.*

CHAPTER FOUR

1 W.W. Warren, *The History of the Ojibway People.*

2 Ibid., 64.

3 P.S. Schmalz, *The Ojibwa of Southern Ontario*, 116.

4 Ibid., 3.

5 Ibid., Introduction.

6 Ibid.

7 P.S. Schmalz, *The Ojibwa of Southern Ontario*, 43–4.

8 A. Henry, *Travels and Adventures in Canada*, 44.

9 P.S. Schmalz, *The Ojibwa of Southern Ontario*, 74.

10 B. Coleman, E. Frogner, E. Eich, *Ojibwa Myths and Legends,*
    55, 56.

11 Ibid.

12 Ibid., 93, 94.

13 Ibid., 56.

14 D. Hodson, "Native Values in a Non-Native World."

15 Ibid., 21.

16 Ibid., 30.

17 Ibid., 31.

18 I. Hallowell, *Culture and Experience*, 161.

19 D. Hodson, "Native Values in a Non-Native World," 39.

20 P.S. Schmalz, *The Ojibwa of Southern Ontario*, 11.

21 Ibid., 43.

CHAPTER FIVE

1 The following observations and reflections about the trauma of the Canadian Native are taken from York's work, other studies, the *Report of the Royal Commission on Aboriginal Peoples* published in 1996, and my own experiences.

2 *Native People* 9, no. 34, 1976.

3 Canada, *Royal Commission*, vol. 1, 13.

4 H. Cardinal, *The Unjust Society*, 25.

5 Canada, *Royal Commission*, vol. 1, 333.

6 P.S. Schmaltz, *The Ojibwa of Southern Ontario*, 147.

7 *Native People* 9, no. 9, 1976.

8 *Native People* 9, no. 44, 1976.

9 H. Cardinal, *The Unjust Society*, 165.

10 "Study of Native Youth in Edmonton," Alberta Deptartment of Culture, Youth and Recreation, 1971.

11 Ibid.

12 G. Manuel and M. Posluns, *The Fourth World: An Indian Reality*.

13 G. York, *The Dispossessed*, 146.

14 Canada, *Royal Commission*, vol. 1, 333-34.

15 G. York, *The Dispossessed*, 23.

16 H. Cardinal, *Unjust Society*.

17 G. York, *The Dispossessed*, 22.

18 Ibid., 36.

19 Canada, *Royal Commission*, vol. 1, 372.

20 Ibid., vol. 3, 603.

21 Ibid., vol. 1, 379.

22 Peter Moon, "Hundreds of Cree and Ojibwa Children Violated."

23 Ibid.

24 Canada, *Royal Commission*, vol. 1, 357.

25 Ibid., vol. 1, 369.

26 Ibid., vol. 1, 372, 373.

27 Ibid.

28 Ibid., 379.

29 Ibid.

30 Ibid.

31 Ibid.

32 Ray Bonisteel, *When the Eagle Landed on the Moon: Circle of Healing*.

33 *Toronto Globe and Mail*, 28 October 2002, A5.

34 G. York, *The Dispossessed*, 44.

35 Ibid.

36 G. Manuel and M. Posluns, *The Fourth World*.

37 *Native People* 9, no. 44 (1976).

38 G. York, *The Dispossessed*, 18.

39 Canada, *Royal Commission*, vol. 3.

40 Ibid., 434.

41 Ibid., 44.

42 Ibid., 159.

43 Quoted in G. York, *The Dispossessed*, 188.

44 Ibid.

45 Newman, *Company of Adventurers*, 190, 113.

46 Canada, *Royal Commission*, vol. 3, 74.

47 H. Smith, *The Religions of Man*, 167.

48 Quoted in ibid., 57.

49 Canada, *Royal Commission*, vol. 3, 54.

50 Ibid., 57.

51 Ibid.

CHAPTER SIX

1 Canada, *Choosing Life*, ix.

2 Ibid., 7, 8.

3 Ibid., 8.

4 J. Ward et al., "Suicide Epidemic among Canadian Indians," 405.

5 Ibid., 47,48.

6 Ibid., 10.

7 A. Pambrun, "Suicide among the Blackfeet Indians."

8 I heard Dr Levine make this remark at a meeting of the Canadian Association for Suicide in Toronto in 1985.

9 *The Concise Oxford Dictionary* describes assimilation as the process by which an outsider, immigrant, or subordinate group becomes "indistinguishably integrated" into a dominant host society.

10 Canada, *Royal Commission*, vol. 4, 156.

11 Ibid., 157.

12 Al Hardy, Robin Mills, circa 1842, in M. Laurence, *The Diviners*, flyleaf.

CHAPTER SEVEN

1 E. Shneidman, *Definitions of Suicide*, 138.

2 Ibid., 139.

3 In B. Rabkin, *Growing Up Dead*, 26.

4 C. Menninger, *Man Against Himself*, 23–71.

5 E. Shneidman, et al., *The Psychology of Suicide*.

6 Ibid., 166.

7 Chart describing accidie or melancholy created by Dr Frank Lake, an English psychiatrist, in *Clinical Theology*.

8 J. White, *The Masks of Melancholy*, 105.

9 C. Menninger, *Man Against Himself*, 21.

10 Ibid., 158.

CHAPTER EIGHT

1 Nishnawbe Aski Nation Youth Forum on Suicide, *Horizons of Hope*, iii.

2 Ibid., viii.

3 Ibid.

4 Ibid., ix.

5 Ibid., 129.

6 Ibid., 10.

7 Ibid., 41.

8 Ibid., 50.

9 Ibid., 106.

10 Ibid.

11 Ibid., 107.

12 Ibid., 57.

13 Ibid., 62.

14 Ibid., 140.

15 Ibid., 143.

16 Ibid.

17 Ibid,. 381.

18 Ibid.

CHAPTER NINE

1 Canada, *Report of the Royal Commission on Aboriginal Peoples*, vol. 1, 647.

2 Canada, *Choosing Life*, 97, 98.

3 Canada, *Royal Commission*, vol. 1, 599.

4 Ibid., 365.

5 C. Hall, G. Lindzey, *Theories of Personality*.

6 Canada, *Royal Commission*, vol. 1, 218.

7 V. Frankl, *Man's Search for Meaning*, 65.

8 Canada, *Royal Commission*, vol. 1, 630.

9 Ibid., 629.

10 Ibid., 663.

11 V. Frankl, *The Doctor and the Soul*, x.

12 Ibid., 63, 64.

13 Ibid., Introduction.

14 Canada, *Royal Commission*.

15 Ibid., vol. 3, 86.

16 Ibid.

CHAPTER TEN

1 R. Corbett, "Unmarked Grave."

2 Ibid., 49.

3 Ibid., 47.

4 Ibid., 49.

5 *Ottawa Saturday Sun*, 28 June 1997, 5.

6 R. Corbett, "Drive to Mark Artist's Grave."

7 A. Akiwenzie, letter, Ottawa Native Concerns Committee, 4 April 1977.

8 Murray Angus, "Chee Chee Remembered."

BIBLIOGRAPHY

Angus, M. "Chee Chee Remembered in Ottawa Ceremony." *Windspeaker*, 8 July 1997.

Baele, N. "Chee Chee's Work Needs No Signature." *Ottawa Citizen*, 15 May 1977.

Bies, E. *Arts West* 5, no. 7 (November/December 1980).

– "The End of the Wild Ride: The Life and Death of Benjamin Chee Chee." Unpublished article, 1980.

Bonisteel, R. *When the Eagle Landed on the Moon: Circle of Healing.* CBC Television, 1989

Brown, F. "A Great Artist." Letter to the Editor, *Ottawa Citizen*, 31 March 1977.

Canada. *Choosing Life: Special Report on Suicide among Aboriginal People.* Ottawa: Canadian Government Publishing 1995.

– *Report of the Royal Commission on Aboriginal Peoples.* 5 vols. Ottawa: Minister of Supply and Services 1996.

Cardinal, H., *The Unjust Society, The Tragedy of Canada's Indians.* Edmonton: Hurtig 1969.

Clark, J., and R. Houle, eds. *Benjamin Chee Chee: The Black Goose Portfolio and Other Works.* Thunder Bay Art Gallery, Thunder Bay, Ont. 1991.

Coleman, B., E. Frogner, and E. Eich. *Ojibwa Myths and Legends.* Minneapolis: Ross and Haines 1962.

Corbett, R. "Unmarked Grave Almost All That's Left of One of Ottawa's Most Prolific Artists." *Ottawa Sunday Sun*, 9 March 1997, 47.

– "Drive to Mark Artist's Grave." *Ottawa Sunday Sun*, 11 March 1997, 5.

Creighton, A. *The Life and Death of Benjamin Chee Chee*. Audio production. CBC Radio 1980.

Edmonstone, W. "The Dying of Chee Chee." *Vancouver Sun*, 1 April 1977.

Fleming, W. *Art, Music, and Ideas*. N.p.: International Thompson Publishing 1970.

Frankl, V. *The Doctor and the Soul*. New York: Knopf 1957.

– *Man's Search for Meaning*. New York: Pocket Books 1963.

Hall, C., and G. Lindzey. *Theories of Personality*. New York: John Wiley & Sons 1978.

Hallowell, I. *Culture and Experience: Collected Essays*. New York: Schuker Books 1955.

Henry, A. *Travels and Adventures in Canada and the Indian Territories in the Years 1760–1776*. Chicago, Ill.: Lakeside Press 1921.

Hodson, D. "Native Values in a Non-Native World." Doctoral dissertation, Department of Education, University of Toronto, 1989.

Lake, F. *Clinical Theology*. London: Dartman, Long and Todd 1966.

Laurence, M. *The Diviners*. Toronto: McClelland & Stewart 1974.

Manuel, G., and M. Posluns. *The Fourth World: An Indian Reality*. Don Mills, Ont.: Macmillan 1974.

McLuhan, E. *Painting and Prints in the Collection of the Thunder Bay National Exhibition Centre and Centre for Indian Art, December 2, 1983 – January 29, 1984*. Thunder Bay Art Gallery, Thunder Bay, Ont. 1991.

Menninger, K. *Man Against Himself.* New York: Harcourt, Brace
     and Co. 1938.

Moon, P. "Hundreds of Cree and Ojibwa Children Violated."
     Toronto Globe and Mail, 19 October 1996.

Native People, vol. 9 (1976), (nos. 9, 24, 34, 44, 46; vol. 10 (1977)
     no. 2. Markham: Alberta Native Communications Society.

Newman, Peter C. *Company of Adventurers: The Story of the
     Hudson's Bay Company.* Markham: Viking 1987.

Nishnawbe Aski Nation Youth Forum on Suicide. *Horizons of
     Hope: An Empowering Journey*: Final Report, Nishnawbe Aski
     Nation Youth Forum on Suicide. Thunder Bay, Ont., 1996.

Pambrun, A. "Suicide among the Blackfeet Indians." *Bulletin
     on Suicidology* 7, 1970.

Platiel, R. "Success of Objibwa Painter Underlines Haunting
     Legacy," *Toronto Globe and Mail,* 30 October 1981.

Rabkin, B. *Growing Up Dead.* Nashville: Abingdon 1975.

Schmalz, P.S. *The Ojibwa of Southern Ontario.* Toronto: University
     of Toronto Press 1991.

Shneidman, E. *Definitions of Suicide.* New York: John Wiley 1985.

Shneidman, E., N. Farberow, and R. Litman. *The Psychology of
     Suicide.* Northvale, N.J.: Jason Aronson 1970.

Smith, H. *The Religions of Man.* New York: Harper 1958.

Ward, J., J. Fox, and A. Evans. "Suicide Epidemic among Canadian
     Indians." *Proceedings of the Ninth International Congress on
     Suicide Prevention and Crisis Intervention.* Helsinki 1977.

Warren, W. *The History of the Ojibway People.* St Paul: Minnesota
     Historical Society Press 1984.

Watson, G. "Portrait of an Artist." *Ottawa Citizen*, 21 March 1977.

White, J. *The Masks of Melancholy*. Downers Grove, Ill.:
   InterVarsity Press 1982.

York, G. *The Dispossessed: Life and Death in Native Canada*.
   Toronto: Lester & Orpen Dennys 1989.

SELECTED BIBLIOGRAPHY ON THE ACT OF SUICIDE

Alexander, V. *In the Wake of Suicide: Stories of the People Left Behind.* San Francisco: Jossey-Bass 1998.

Barrett, T. *Life after Suicide: The Survivor's Grief Experience.* Fargo, N.D.: Aftermath Research 1989.

Berman, A., and D. Jobes. *Adolescent Suicide Assessment and Intervention.* Washington, D.C.: American Psychological Association 1991. Atlanta: Bolton Press 1984.

Durkheim, E. *Suicide: A Study in Sociology.* New York: Free Press 1951.

Farberow, N.L., ed. *The Many Faces of Suicide.* New York: McGraw-Hill 1980.

Fusé, T. *Suicide, Individual and Society.* Toronto: Canadian Scholars Press 1997.

Grollman, E. *Suicide, Prevention, Intervention.* Boston: Beacon Press 1951.

Hawton, K., and K. Van Heeringen, eds. *The International Handbook of Suicide and Attempted Suicide.* New York: John Wiley & Sons 2000.

Klagsbrun, F. *Too Young to Die: Youth and Suicide.* Boston: Houghton Mifflin 1976.

Lester, D. *Suicidal Prevention: Resources for the Millenium.* London and New York: Taylor & Francis 2001.

Maris, R., A. Berman, J.T. Maltsberger, and R. Yufit, eds. *Assessement and Prevention of Suicide*. New York: Guilford Press 1992.

Mishara, B.L., ed. *The Impact of Suicide*. New York: Springer Publishing 1995.

Nishnawbe Aski Nation Youth Forum on Suicide. *Horizons of Hope: An Empowering Journey*. Final Report (P.O. Box 755 Stn. F, Fort William Reserve, R.R. 4, Mission Road, Thunder Bay, Ont. P7C 4W6) 1996.

Peck, M., N. Farberow, and R. Litman. *Youth Suicide*. New York: Springer 1985.

Perlin, S., ed. *A Handbook for the Study of Suicide*. New York: Oxford University Press 1975.

Rabkin, B. *Growing Up Dead*. Nashville: Abingdon 1975.

Shneidman, E. *The Suicidal Mind*. New York: Oxford University Press 1996.

– *Definitions of Suicide*. New York: John Wiley & Sons 1985.

Ward, J., J. Fox, and A. Evans. "Suicide and the Canadian Natives: Suicide among Canadian Natives." *Proceedings, Ninth International Congress on Suicide Prevention and Crisis Intervention, Helsinki, 1977*.

White, T.W. *How to Identify Suicidal People: A Systematic Approach to Risk Assessment*. Philadelphia: Charles Press 1999.

INDEX

vigil, 7, 8

Ward, John, xvi, xvii, 9, 97, 98,
    103, 126
Warren, William W., 43, 44, 46, 48
Watt, Dorothy, 17, 19
White, John, 122
white race and culture, 11, 63, 65,
    109, 143
Wikwemikong Reserve, xvi, 103,
    105, 106, 126

York, Geoffrey, 62, 69, 71, 81, 88–9